This introduction to the early horn provides an historical account of the instrument's development during the eighteenth and nineteenth centuries as well as a practical guide to playing techniques and principles of interpretation. The book aims to help performers to play in an historically appropriate style and to guide listeners towards a clearer understanding of the issues which affected the way the horn was played during the period. It includes chapters on the historical background of the instrument, its design and development, and choice of instrument today. A series of case studies which include the music of Bach, Haydn, Mozart, Beethoven, Schubert, Schumann and Brahms, will help performers to make a well-grounded, period interpretation of major works from the horn repertoire. Complemented by an extensive bibliography this accessible guide will appeal to players of all levels.

JOHN HUMPHRIES is a horn player and teacher. He has arranged many works for publication, performance and recording. His editions of Rosetti's horn concertos and his reconstructions of Mozart's incomplete horn concerto movements have been recorded by leading performers.

Cambridge Handbooks to the Historical Performance of Music

GENERAL EDITORS Colin Lawson and Robin Stowell

During the last three decades historical performance has become part of mainstream musical life. However, there is as yet no one source from which performers and students can find an overview of the significant issues or glean practical information pertinent to a particular instrument. This series of handbooks guides the modern performer towards the investigation and interpretation of evidence found both in early performance treatises and in the mainstream repertory. Books on individual instruments contain chapters on historical background, equipment, technique and musical style and are illustrated by case studies of significant works in the repertoire. An introductory book provides a more general survey of issues common to all areas of historical performance and will also inform a wide range of students and music lovers.

Published titles

The Historical Performance of Music: An Introduction
COLIN LAWSON AND ROBIN STOWELL

The Early Clarinet: A Practical Guide
COLIN LAWSON

The Early Horn: A Practical Guide
JOHN HUMPHRIES

Early Keyboard Instruments, 1550–1900: A Practical Guide
DAVID ROWLAND

Forthcoming

The Early Violin and Viola: A Practical Guide
ROBIN STOWELL

The Early Flute: A Practical Guide
RACHEL BROWN

The Early Horn
A Practical Guide

JOHN HUMPHRIES

CAMBRIDGE
UNIVERSITY PRESS

PUBLISHED BY THE PRESS SYNDICATE OF THE UNIVERSITY OF CAMBRIDGE
The Pitt Building, Trumpington Street, Cambridge, United Kingdom

CAMBRIDGE UNIVERSITY PRESS
The Edinburgh Building, Cambridge CB2 2RU, UK   www.cup.cam.ac.uk
40 West 20th Street, New York NY 10011-4211, USA   www.cup.org
10 Stamford Road, Oakleigh, Melbourne 3166, Australia
Ruiz de Alarcón 13, 28014 Madrid, Spain

© John Humphries 2000

First published 2000

Printed in the United Kingdom at the University Press, Cambridge

Typeface 10.25/14 Adobe Minion   *System* QuarkXPress™   [SE]

A catalogue record for this book is available from the British Library

Library of Congress cataloguing in publication data

ISBN 0 521 63210 2 hardback
ISBN 0 521 63559 4 paperback

For Elizabeth and Michael

Contents

List of illustrations   viii
Acknowledgements   ix

1   **Introduction**   1

2   **Historical background**   7

3   **Equipment**   27

4   **Technique**   51

5   **The language of musical style**   68

6   **Case studies**   80
   Bach: Quoniam from Mass in B minor, BWV232   80
   Haydn: Concerto in D, Hob.VIId: 3 *and*
      attrib. Haydn: Concerto in D, Hob.VIId: 4   82
   Mozart: Concerto in E♭, K495   86
   Beethoven: Sonata in F, op. 17   89
   Schubert: Auf dem Strom, D943   93
   Schumann: Adagio and Allegro in A♭, op. 70   97
   Brahms: Trio in E♭, op. 40   99

Notes   104
Bibliography   120
Index   129

Illustrations

1 Inventionshorn by F. Korn, Mainz, *c.* 1825–30   *page* 29

2 Orchestral horn by Halary, Paris, *c.* 1830   30

3 Horn with 3 Périnet valves and sauterelle (detachable valve section). Illustration taken from 1898 catalogue for *L'Association Générale des Ouvriers*   33

4 Horn with 2 Stölzel valves. Illustration taken from the cover of the English translation of Charles Gounod's *Méthode de Cor à pistons*   37

5 Typical German-style, nineteenth-century rotary-valved horn with fixed mouthpipe. Illustration taken from Hugo Riemann's *Catechism of Musical Instruments* (1888)   40

6a Typical modern mouthpiece   43

6b Typical nineteenth-century mouthpiece   43

7 Chromatic mute for a hand horn, shown in Adam Wirth's *Praktische, systematisch geordnete Hornschule* (1877)   46

8 Frontispiece from *The Compleat Tutor* (London: John Simpson, 1746)   53

Acknowledgements

I have greatly enjoyed writing this book, not least because it has given me the opportunity to discuss ideas and problems with a wide range of friends and colleagues whose insight I respect. They, in turn, have been unfailingly generous with both ideas and information, and I particularly appreciate the support and interest of Keith Burdett, Anthony Catterick, Farquharson Cousins, Bradley Strauchen, Viola Roth, Trevor Herbert, Robert Paxman, Enrico Weller, Timothy Brown, Marshall Stoneham, Peter Ricketts and Katy Edge. Michael Thompson kindly lent me material over a longer period than he can possibly have anticipated, and as well as taking immense care over proof-reading the draft manuscript; Anthony Halstead and Kjell Moseng took a personal interest in its content, answering innumerable questions and volunteering a number of valuable suggestions. I am also grateful to Barry Tuckwell for his encouragement, to St John's College, Oxford for giving me the opportunity to return to the University as a participant in their excellent vacation study scheme, and to Hélène la Rue and Joanna Archibald for giving me access to the resources of the Bate Collection. The staff of the British Library, the Bodleian Library, Westminster City Council's Central Music Library, Paxman Ltd, and Gebr. Alexander of Mainz were equally helpful, while Penny Souster of Cambridge University Press, and the series editors, Colin Lawson and Robin Stowell, have been patience itself.

Finally, I should like to thank my wife, Margaret, who has found time to be deeply involved in every aspect of the book's creation and also compiled the index. Without her it would never have been written.

John Humphries

1 Introduction

The twentieth century has seen an immense number of changes in performance practice. Listen, for example, to Elgar's recordings of his own orchestral works with the London Symphony Orchestra and the Royal Albert Hall Orchestra in the 1920s and thirties. The woodwind play without vibrato, the narrow-bore trombones are incisive and penetrating but never over-assertive and the single F horns' sound is reticent and pure-toned. These are authentic performances which reveal the substantial difference between the sounds which Elgar heard as he composed and conducted, and those which we hear in the same works today. Modern performances may be technically slicker, but they are often far removed from the style of the originals, and present the music in a way which Elgar cannot possibly have imagined.

They also reveal something of the difficulty of interpreting historic music, for while Mahler carefully marked all the strings' portamenti in the score of his 4th symphony (1901; rev. 1906), none appears in Elgar's orchestral writing. It would be easy to conclude from their absence that, by the 1920s, portamenti had fallen out of fashion, but it is clear from his recordings that by now they were so characteristic of string playing that they no longer needed to be notated. The lack of recordings from earlier periods makes it very much more difficult to capture the unnotated essence of eighteenth- and nineteenth-century music today, so players who wish to give well-informed and historically aware performances need to be familiar with the history of the instrument itself, the equipment which was available or preferred in different times and places, players' techniques and musical style in general.

The history of the Early Music Movement
Although a few earlier musicians had shown an interest in the music of the past, the first seeds of interest in playing music on historically

appropriate instruments, and in a style which its composer would have recognised, germinated at the beginning of the twentieth century. These pio-
neers were concerned with music which far precedes the arrival of the horn
in the concert hall, however, and works from later periods only began to
attract the interest of their successors in the 1960s.

'Early Music' has been able to develop because, since the end of the first
world war, audiences have, for the first time, taken more interest in the
music of the past than the work of their contemporaries. Nevertheless, until
the 1960s, most people seemed content for earlier music to be played on
modern instruments, and it is only during the last forty years that musicians
have begun to experiment with period instruments and the phrasing, articulation, balance, texture and tempi which are appropriate to the time when
the work was composed. At first, the results were often disappointing: the art
of making reproduction instruments was in its infancy, and with little experience of using them, players often gave pallid performances in their efforts
to avoid any hint of Romantic excess. As such they posed little threat to the
status quo, but during the 1970s and 80s a wave of performers began to
prove that historical performances could be vibrant and personal as well as
historically informed, and major record companies began to issue recordings using original instruments.

Today, standards of performance and scholarship are so well developed
that resistance to authentic performances has all but crumbled, and with
greater confidence has come a more enlightened approach to repertoire.
While authentic performances once stopped at the middle of the eighteenth
century, some period orchestras today include Brahms and Wagner on a
regular basis, and Arnold Dolmetsch's pioneering work on the performance
of sixteenth-century music is now so far removed from current mores that it
is considered worthy of historic study in its own right. He worked in interesting times, for while three pioneer revivalist viola da gamba players are
listed in the 1910 edition of the *Musical Directory, Annual and Almanack*,[1]
the same publication lists two players of the ophicleide, the nineteenth-
century bass brass instrument which was then still part of a living tradition
but, having been superseded by the tuba, is now studied as an authentic
instrument.[2]

Historical awareness

Oral tradition

The hand horn era is, likewise, remarkably close to our own time. The Paris Conservatoire stopped teaching the hand horn only in 1903 – just two years before Arnold Dolmetsch made his first recorder – and in 1910 Otto Langey commented that 'Some old players are still opposed to the entire use of valves because, they argue, that the character of the original sound suffers in consequence.'[3] Indeed, it was not until the 1930s that the double horn was regarded as anything more than a curiosity in England, and, even today, right hand position is directly influenced by best hand horn practice. Many older players are happy to reminisce about the characteristics of F horns, for most will have used them, and even played them professionally, in their youth. Some may also have known others who studied the hand horn as part of a living tradition: players in the London area speak warmly of Handel Knott, who learned the hand horn from his father and played professionally before opting for a career in the insurance industry.

Recordings

As well as the orchestral recordings by Elgar and his contemporaries, there is also a small, but significant number of recordings which show how the horn was played as a solo instrument. The flexible, lyrical tone quality which is revealed by Edouard Vuillermoz's 1929 performance of Emile Vuillermoz's 'Pièce Mélodique',[4] is quite different from the strident vibrato which is often associated with French playing from the 1930s to the 1960s. Other very different sounding recordings include the LSO playing Weber's 'Oberon' and 'Freischütz' overtures under Nikisch in July 1914, when the first horn was probably Thomas Busby. Karl Stiegler took part in a recording of Mendelssohn's 'Hunter's Farewell' in an arrangement for four Vienna horns before 1910, and the technique and panâche of today's finest virtuosi are rivalled by the magnificent 1912 performance of the 'Siegfried Horn Call', by Friedrich Gumbert's pupil, Anton Horner.[5]

Sadly, there are no recordings of the hand horn being played as part of a living tradition. A tape survives of Dennis Brain playing Mozart's D major Concerto K412/514 during the 1950s on a hand horn by L.J. Raoux, but while he was instinctively brilliant on the instrument, he would never have claimed specialist knowledge of performance practice beyond what he had learned by playing a Raoux-Labbaye single F horn. Alan Civil and Hermann Baumann were the first serious modern exponents of the hand horn, giving a number of pioneering performances both in concert and on recordings, but today's young British specialists owe a great deal to Anthony Halstead, the first modern top-class player in England to play almost exclusively on the hand horn.

Retrospective publications

One of the first to develop a serious academic interest in the horn was W.F.H. Blandford, a professional zoologist who published a number of very influential papers on the instrument, and whose voluminous correspondence with Reginald Morley-Pegge is preserved in Oxford University's Bate Collection.[6] Morley-Pegge's book, *The French Horn*,[7] added significantly to Blandford's work and is vital reading for any horn player with aspirations to authenticity. Scholarship has moved on in some respects, but Morley-Pegge is hardly ever wrong, and the insight which he gained as a pupil of both Brémond and Vuillermoz, and as a musicologist, professional performer and amateur hand horn player in Paris, gave him an invaluable understanding of the French tutors. His account of developments in Germany and Austria is less complete, but he was also a philanthropist, and today the Bate Collection is home to his magnificent collections of horns and rare tutors. Birchard Coar's *Critical Study of the Nineteenth Century Horn Virtuosi in France*[8] contains a considerable amount of information from the French tutors but, like his other book, *The French Horn*,[9] is out of print, and copies are difficult to find.

Hans Pizka's *Dictionary for Hornists*[10] covers the German-speaking countries in more detail, and in *The Horn and Horn Playing and the Austro-Bohemian Tradition, 1680–1830*,[11] Horace Fitzpatrick covers some esoteric ground which is not included in other works. Two books by Bernhard Brüchle and Kurt Janetzky, *A Pictorial History of the Horn*[12] and *The Horn*,[13] are worth consulting, and Robin Gregory's *The Horn: A Comprehensive Guide to the Modern Instrument and its Music*,[14] is particularly helpful for its repertoire lists. Barry Tuckwell's volume in the series of Yehudi Menuhin Music Guides[15] and Jeremy Montagu's book, *The French Horn*,[16] are also useful, while Anthony Baines' *Brass Instruments*,[17] and the *Cambridge*

Companion to Brass Instruments,[18] are essential reading for serious horn students. Among the most useful periodicals are back numbers of the *Journal of the Historic Brass Society*, the *Galpin Society Journal*, *Brass Bulletin* and *Horn Call*, the journal of the International Horn Society.

Instruments

Until the 1970s, most players used the term 'hand horn' indiscriminately to refer equally to Baroque and Classical instruments, and few attempted to understand the differences between their technique. We now know more about the distinction between the two, but the lack of good reproduction nineteenth-century instruments means that performance practice from the period is still under-researched. Horn-making is never big business even for those making contemporary instruments, and as the distinguished nineteenth-century London maker William Brown explained to Blandford, the work was so skilled that he did 'practically all of it himself, whereas he could give out jobs on other instruments'.[19] Today's limited horn market is substantially smaller for those making reproduction instruments, and the incentive to set up the precision tools needed to build a copy of an early valved instrument is very slight indeed.

Contemporary writers

The relatively few eighteenth-century accounts of horn playing technique are examined in chapter 4, but their practical advice is limited, so it is fortunate that reasonably competent valve horn players can deduce by trial and error much of the basic technical set-up required to play the early horn. Those who want to play at a more advanced level have problems, however, and while the concertos by Mozart, Haydn, Rosetti and Punto, and the Sonata, op. 17 by Beethoven, were written for players who were familiar with hand stopping, they were composed before any detailed account of the technique appeared in print. The high point in horn literature – and one of the finest and most thorough instruction books written for any instrument – is the *Méthode de Cor Alto et Cor Basse*[20] by Louis Dauprat. Written as part of a series of tutors which were published in connection with the work of the Paris Conservatoire, this is exclusively for hand horn players, and with the recent publication of an English translation it is now available to non-French speakers for the first time. Meifred's *Méthode pour le Cor*

Chromatique,[21] attempts to redress the balance in favour of the nineteenth-century valve horn, but was written as an adjunct to Dauprat's *Méthode*, not as a separate work.

The only native Englishman to write a tutor in the nineteenth century was Charles Tully[22] but a small number of other works were available in translation, and such works are invaluable to modern players' study of period performance. There will always be an audience for a soloist of sensitive artistry and brilliant technique on the modern horn, regardless of whether he plays Bach, Mozart, Brahms or Ligeti, but, as global uniformity of sound becomes the norm, we should cherish the diverse palette of tone colours which are characteristic of historic instruments.

2   Historical Background

In his autobiography, *Those Twentieth Century Blues*,[1] Sir Michael Tippett recalls writing for electric guitar in the 1960s and 1970s in his operas, 'The Knot Garden' and 'The Ice Break'. 'Finding a player who could cope with the part was almost impossible. You either used an acoustic guitarist who could read accurately but had limited knowledge of the special sonorities of the electric instrument, or you engaged a rock musician, whose variable reading and inexperience at playing to a conductor's beat placed the security of the ensemble at risk.'

The introduction of the horn to the concert hall must have posed a similar chicken-and-egg problem. While the instrument's main rôle was on the hunting field, players had no need to read music, and so composers had few opportunities to discover its potential. With little music available for them to play, horn players could not make a living as professionals, there was no incentive to extend their technique, and composers remained ill-at-ease with the instrument as part of the orchestra. Tradition has it that the horn's first appearance in notated music is the little fanfare in Cavalli's 'Le Nozze de Teti e di Peleo' (1639),[2] but after this there were no further significant developments until Count Franz Anton Sporck[3] heard the newly invented cor de chasse at Versailles during his Grand Tour in the 1680s.

1700–1750

Sporck, a wealthy nobleman from Lissa in Bohemia (now Leszno, Poland), was so taken with the horn that he sent two of his retainers, Wenzel Sweda and Peter Röllig, to learn to play it in Paris. As the retainer of one of the greatest hunting establishments of the period, Sporck's main interest was in the outdoor potential of the horn, but he was also a dedicated musician who ran the first opera troupe in Bohemia and an orchestra which played at Prague and Kuks, north of Hradec Králové,[4] as well as Lissa. It is said that horns began to appear in his ensemble music at a very early stage, but none of the court's surviving repertoire features the instrument, and his real legacy lies in the rôle he played in bringing the art of horn playing to Central Europe and possibly in inspiring Nuremberg's brass makers to begin to build horns in the 1680s. It is not clear whether he had any direct connection with the first recorded use of horns as an integral part of the orchestra, a performance of Carlo Agostino Badia's opera, 'Diana rappacificata con Venere e con Amore', which was staged in Vienna in 1700,[5] but by now others were also thinking of including horns in their scores: they reappear only five years later in Reinhard Keiser's opera, 'Octavia', and from 1712 were used regularly by Christoph Graupner[6] in Darmstadt.

J.S. Bach

The most celebrated of the Saxon composers who first used the horn on a regular basis was J.S. Bach, who in 1713 included the instrument in his Weimar cantata 'Was mir behagt' (BWV 208). He then used it again in Brandenburg Concerto no. 1 (BWV 1046), a work based on movements which he had written in Weimar but which he put together in Cöthen and probably intended for particular visiting performers. With his move to Leipzig, however, he began to write for horns on a more regular basis, suggesting that local players were available in the city. These were probably primarily trumpeters, and would therefore have been quite at home with the high tessitura which composers had to use if they were to write melodically for the Baroque horn.

Bach's Leipzig works for horn range in scale from the two tiny obbligatos in the 'Peasant' Cantata (BWV 212, 1742), to extended cantata movements for pairs of horns in F, such as the opening choruses of 'Wie schön leuchtet der Morgenstern' (BWV 1, 1725) and part four of the *Christmas Oratorio* (BWV 248, 1735). In 'Wär Gott nicht mit uns diese Zeit' (BWV 14, 1735), the extraordinarily difficult obbligato for horn in B♭ alto ascends to the eighteenth harmonic, but Bach's best known obbligato for the instrument is the Quoniam from the Mass in B minor (BWV 232). All of these parts limit themselves almost entirely to the notes of the harmonic series, but Bach also wrote a number of other works where the solo 'horn' line is written at concert pitch and includes many chromatic notes which are not possible on the Baroque horn as we know it. His players may have had some rudimentary knowledge of hand stopping, but it is possible that in writing for 'corno', Bach envisaged an instrument which is not like the horn we know. The first movement of the cantata, 'Also hat Gott die Welt geliebt' (BWV 68, 1725), for example, includes an extended obbligato in D minor for 'corno'. Here, this may be an abbreviation for 'cornetto', an instrument which he uses in the finale chorale of the cantata, but the term also appears elsewhere: 'Halt im Gedächtnis Jesum Christ' (BWV 67, 1724) includes a 'Corno da tirarsi' ('slide horn') which is also at times abbreviated to 'corno' and was apparently capable of playing notes which are quite impossible on a natural horn unless it is hand stopped. No such instrument survives, but some trumpets seem to have had slides as early as the fifteenth century, and the 'Tromba da tirarsi' ('slide trumpet') also appears in Bach's scores. Other instruments which he specifies include 'Corne par force', 'Corno da caccia', 'Corne de chasse' and 'Lituus', but while these may have described different designs of horn, particularly at a time when it was developing rapidly, they may also have been used to distinguish different ways of holding it. As Morley-Pegge wrote in 1960,[7] 'Until fresh evidence is available we can only hazard a guess.'

Dresden

The situation in Bach's Leipzig was quite different from that in Dresden, where the Trumpeters' Guild forbade its members to double on the horn. As a result a separate school of horn players developed, bringing with it opportunities for low horn players to experiment with rudimentary hand stopping by as early as 1717.[8] Evidence that the city's players boasted a virtuoso technique contemporary with and after Bach can be seen in the work of composers such as Johann Heinichen, Jan Zelenka and Johann Hasse, and in an extraordinary collection of concertos and chamber works for horn solo which survives in Lund University, Sweden.[9] Written by composers who seem to have worked in the Dresden area in the first half of the eighteenth century, this collection includes two very attractive pieces for a high horn player by J.J. Quantz, and others by Christoph Förster, one of the Graun brothers, and a composer named Reinhardt whose work calls for a very athletic technique. There are also works by some of the Dresden horn players themselves, including a concerto by Johann Knechtel, who replaced Johann Schindler in the court orchestra in 1734,[10] and an anonymous piece which may be the work of Anton Hampel.[11]

Hampel and Haudek

Hampel, who specialised in playing low horn lines, joined the Dresden court orchestra in 1737, when he replaced Andreas Schindler. Both he and his younger colleague, the high horn player Karl Haudek, were born in Bohemia – Hampel in Prague and Haudek in Dobříš – and both moved to Dresden when they were about twenty-seven years old,[12] staying there for the rest of their lives and earning distinguished reputations both as duettists and teachers. They both also taught Giovanni Punto, and the appointment of Punto's own pupil, Heinrich Domnich, to the post of horn professor at the Paris Conservatoire in 1795 ensured that the Saxon/Bohemian tradition of playing would have a major effect on horn playing in France in the nineteenth century.

Hampel also probably played an important part in the development of the Inventionshorn and the non-transposing mute,[13] and although he was probably not alone in experimenting with the use of the hand in the bell in the mid-eighteenth century, his immortality was assured when Domnich credited him as its sole inventor in 1807.[14] The first time Hampel tried imitating oboists' habit of quietening their instruments by stuffing a cloth in the bell, Domnich writes, 'he was surprised to find that the pitch of his instrument rose by a semitone. In a flash of inspiration he realised that by alternately inserting and withdrawing the cotton plug he could cover without a break every diatonic and chromatic scale. He thereupon composed some new music for the horn that included notes hitherto foreign to the instrument. Soon afterwards, finding that the plug could be replaced advantageously by his hand alone, he discarded the plug altogether.' While this is clearly an oversimplified version of the process, and particularly of the way in which the pitch is changed, the passages which Morley-Pegge quotes from Hampel's compositions leave no doubt that he knew how to hand stop. The anonymous piece which is attributed to Hampel in the Lund University Collection also demands the technique – it includes, for example, a two-octave descending scale written in G major – and some of its figuration is said to recall the content of his manuscript book of exercises, 'Lection pro Cornui',[15] which was lost in the second world war. Another example of early hand stopping can be found in a volume of Haudek's duets which recently reappeared in West London,[16] suggesting that, if Hampel ever regarded hand stopping as his own invention, it was not one which he was afraid to share with his colleague.

Handel, Telemann, Vivaldi

Saxony also influenced the development of horn playing elsewhere in Europe during the first half of the century. Handel, who was born in the area, was the first to write for the horn in England (Water Music, *c.* 1717) and although he never expects the extreme levels of virtuosity which were required by some of his contemporaries back at home, there must have been someone in London who could cope with difficult parts like the obbligato in the aria 'Va tacito' (*Giulio Cesare*, 1724). Telemann, who had both studied and worked in Leipzig, also wrote a number of works for the horn in the course of his travels, and it is possible that Vivaldi was influenced in his use of the instrument by his pupil, the Dresden violinist, J.G. Pisendel.

1750–1800

The changes which took place in musical style in the mid-eighteenth century had a fundamental effect on the rôle of the horn, for as orchestral textures acquired a new significance, composers began to realise that, as well as playing high, florid clarino parts, it could also blend with wind, strings and voices, binding an orchestral or chamber texture together with middle-register held notes. Consequently, from about 1760 most orchestral and wind ensemble music called for a pair of horns, with one player specialising in higher parts ('cor alto') and the other in lower ones ('cor basse'). This greatly increased employment opportunities, but while hand stopping soon became a vital part of the soloist's technique, its almost complete omission from orchestral parts – regardless of the quality of the players – is one of the most striking features of horn writing in the second half of the century.

Leutgeb and Punto

The careers of the contemporaries Giovanni Punto and Joseph Leutgeb tell us a great deal about horn playing in the second half of the eighteenth century, for Punto travelled extensively, had an international reputation, and left a permanent mark on the profession through his teaching, while Leutgeb is known today mainly in connection with Mozart's concertos.

Leutgeb met Leopold, Wolfgang's father, when he joined the orchestra of the Prince-Archbishop of Salzburg in about 1763, and remained in touch with the family when he moved back to his native Vienna in 1777 to run his father-in-law's business. Although he was probably never in the front rank of contemporary virtuosi he was certainly a fine and musical player whose real talent lay, according to the *Mercure de France*, not in pyrotechnics but in his 'ability to deliver a singing adagio as musically and as accurately as the most mellow voice'.[17] Mozart never asks him to attempt the virtuoso lines which his contemporaries often required, no portrait of him survives, and we can only surmise that he would have played a Bohemian instrument, but the length of his relationship with Mozart gives us a fascinating overview of the way in which his age seems to have affected his technique (see chapter 6).

In contrast, Giovanni Punto, the cor basse player for whom Beethoven wrote his horn sonata, spent much of his life as a travelling virtuoso, and as the most celebrated of all eighteenth-century horn players, demonstrated the art of hand stopping throughout Europe. Undeterred by the French Revolution, he eventually settled in Paris, but was born in Zehušice, some seventy-five miles to the east of Prague, in 1746, and changed his name from Stich after escaping serfdom. He took lessons with Hampel and Haudek, and in 1768 started travelling Europe, visiting England twice in the 1770s, and making a particular impression on Fröhlich for his dynamic control, varied tone colour, astonishing articulation and a silvery bright tone, which was 'foreign to any of his predecessors.'[18] The anonymous author of the *New Instructions*,[19] however, was unimpressed by his hand stopping: 'Mr Ponto ... constantly uses this method, by which means the half tones are expressed, which is not to be done by any other method: but it is deemed by Judges of the Horn that the principal beauty, the tone, is greatly impaired thereby.' Charles Burney was equally unconvinced: 'with all his dexterity, [he] produced some of these new notes with similar difficulty to a person ridden by the night mare, who tries to cry out but cannot'.[20] In Punto's defence, however, others embraced hand stopping with alacrity: on hearing Spandau play a concerto at Covent Garden, Hawkins commented that, although some of the work was in C minor, 'all the intervals seemed to be as perfect as in any wind instrument; this improvement was effected by putting his right hand into the bottom or bell of the instrument, and attempering the sounds by the application of his fingers to different parts of the tube.'[21]

Esterházy

The Esterházy family had enjoyed the services of a series of fine horn players even before they attracted Haydn to the court in 1761, and on 9 April 1763 the two-horn section of Johannes Knoblauch and Thaddäus Steinmüller was joined by Carl Franz, a virtuoso who was renowned for his four-octave range and for whom Haydn probably wrote the brilliant 'Divertimento a tre' for horn, violin and cello. The arrival of Franz Reiner in the following August meant that Haydn had an outstanding quartet at his disposal, and by the end of the year he had composed both a Cassation for four concertante horns and strings, and the Symphony known today as no. 72 in D. Reiner left shortly afterwards, however, and it was only when Johann May and Franz Stamitz were appointed after Knoblauch's death in 1765 that Haydn again had a section of four horns.[22] This time the result was the 'Hornsignal' symphony, no. 31 in D, which contains virtuoso passages for all four players, and a number of other works including the symphonies no. 48 in C and 51 in B♭ which tax them to their limits.

Schwabia: Oettingen-Wallerstein

Music was also greatly enjoyed at the court of Oettingen-Wallerstein at Harburg, and between 1745 and 1766 Franz Pokorny wrote a number of concertos and symphonies to feature the playing of the horn players Friedrich Domnich – the father of Heinrich – and Johann Türrschmidt. The accession of Count Kraft Ernst in 1773 gave a further boost to the court's music, and his appointments included the excellent horn players Josef Nagel, Franz Zwierzina and Carl, son of Johann, Türrschmidt.[23] Antonio Rosetti, the court's Kapellmeister and the best known of its distinguished composers, took full advantage of this, writing some extremely demanding concertos for them to play, and dedicating at least one of his six surviving double horn concertos to Nagel and Zwierzina.

Chamber music: eighteenth century

Duets for two horns had been popular since at least 1733, when John Walsh, the London publisher, printed *Forrest Harmony*,[24] a *Collection of the most Celebrated Aires, Minuets and Marches; Together with Curious Pieces out of the Water Musick, made on purpose for two French Horns By the Greatest Masters*. Further collections of duets include a manuscript set in a volume marked 'Andrew Wallace' and dated 1 July 1754,[25] and *Twelve Duettos for two French Horns or two German Flutes* (1757), by the celebrated horn player, 'Mr Charles'.[26] It is tempting to think that the 'Mr Humple' who contributed to a collection of duets with 'some trios or club pieces' could have been Hampel,[27] and difficult to imagine what inspired Valentine Holmes of Chelsea to write the 24 duets for two horns or guitars which were published by Jonathan Fentum in 1764.[28] This unlikely choice of alternative instruments is also found in William Bates' eighteen Duettinos which were published for two guitars, two French Horns or two clarinets by Longman in about 1770.[29]

Horn duets were also being published in Continental Europe by the middle of the century, providing repertoire for the many pairs of players who were now increasingly employed in court orchestras. Travelling duet-tists also enjoyed great popularity, and on 2 March 1786 Carl Türrschmidt and Johann Palsa appeared together with their silver Raoux horns at one of Salomon's London subscription concerts.[30] They also published fifty duets as their Opus 3 in 1795, but the best known of the many which were com-posed before the turn of the century are Mozart's K487. The authorship of three of the twelve is confirmed by surviving manuscripts, but the extreme tessitura of some of the remainder is quite unlike anything else which Mozart wrote for the horn and has led some writers to question their authenticity.

There are few examples of works for three or more horns until the early nineteenth century, when they became particularly popular in Paris. Reicha's trios op. 82 are the most commonly played today, but Dauprat also wrote for three and four horns, and was not alone in writing his Grand Sextet, for three others by Bedřich Weber, the director of the Prague Conservatory, were written to exploit the potential of the valve horns which had been brought to the city from Vienna by Joseph Kail. In general, however, modern horn players' enthusiasm for works for large numbers of horns is mainly the product of twentieth-century compositions and arrangements.

The horn's developing orchestral rôle also began to assure it a place in chamber music with other instruments, and although Mozart's Quintet in E♭, K407 is perhaps pre-eminent in the repertoire for horn and strings, other challenging works include Beethoven's delightful Sextet for two horns and strings, op. 81b, Punto's Quartets for horn and strings and, from early in the nineteenth century, Reicha's Quintet in E, op. 106.

The horn appears more commonly, however, in chamber music with other wind instruments, for from about 1760 until at least the 1830s Central European courts often retained a 'Harmonie', a small band of wind players which usually comprised pairs of horns and bassoons with two clarinets and/or oboes. Such groups were required to play at a variety of functions – most notably during dinner – and while Mozart probably intended his E♭ Serenade, K375, and his C minor Serenade, K388, for the Harmonie at the court of the Viennese Emperor, his works, and those by Haydn and Beethoven, are only the tip of a vast surviving, but largely unpublished, iceberg.[31] Franz Krommer's works have a particular attraction for the horn player, for he often takes the trouble to give the second horn a real chance to shine, and even allows it to sound the first subject in the first movement of the Partita in E♭, op. 69. Only a few of the thirteen partitas which he published at the beginning of the nineteenth century have been reprinted, however, and about fifteen more remain in manuscript. The repertoire often calls for a surprisingly high technical standard: another Partita in E♭, which is attributed to Krommer but is more probably by the shadowy 'Signor Schoen'[32] is effectively a virtuoso concerto for two horns accompanied by wind sextet.

As well as playing original music for wind the Harmonies also specialised in playing transcriptions of other works, and although unauthorised arrangements exist of Haydn's *The Creation*, Mozart's Horn Quintet, K407, and Beethoven's 'Pathétique' Sonata op. 13, as well as symphonies by all three composers, most of the works arranged for Harmonie come from operas. A transcription of *Die Entführung aus dem Serail* is thought by some to be by Mozart himself, but most were the work of professional arrangers, and Beethoven authorised one of the most prolific, Wenzel Sedlak, to transcribe *Fidelio*. Such commissions were often intended to increase the number of people who would hear the work, and it was usual to arrange quite substantial sections, including the overture and a series of arias.

Nineteenth century

The context in which horn players worked began to change at the beginning of the nineteenth century: a number of instruction books were published, orchestral parts began to require their players to hand stop, the popularity of travelling horn soloists suddenly waned, and with the Industrial Revolution came the technology which allowed the invention of valves.

In retrospect, the obvious reaction to the invention of valves would have been for both players and composers to abandon hand stopping as soon as possible. As Friedrich Schneider wrote in AMZ in 1817,[33] 'How solo-horn playing will benefit from this invention is easy to imagine: one only has to think of the eternal monotony of passages played on the horn in concert music up to the present.' But instead the battle for the supremacy of the valve horn over the hand horn was to be hard fought, and while valves made some inroads straight away, many players and composers preferred the hand horn for a very long time indeed. France was particularly slow to change over, accepting the valve horn unequivocally only in 1903, but English players also showed considerable reluctance to change, and while some German players adapted to it very quickly, its dominance was far from total for some time. Indeed, in some places outside Europe, the hand horn survived well into the twentieth century: W.F.H. Blandford's cousin heard it played in an orchestra in Goa in about 1920.[34]

The horn was only one of many instruments whose development was greatly affected by the Industrial Revolution. The piano, previously a relatively soft-toned instrument, suddenly became immensely powerful, perfect for virtuoso display in large concert halls and capable of battling with orchestras which themselves were increasing in both size and volume. The violin and its technique also changed considerably, and both instruments could now offer an intensity of tone which was ideally suited to the sustained ideas which Romantic composers developed over extended time-frames. Both were played by performers whose personality attracted at least as much attention as their extraordinary technical ability: Franz Liszt headed an army of virtuoso keyboard players who captured the hearts and minds of audiences throughout Europe, and the glamour and mystery which surrounded Nicolò Paganini endowed the violin with an exoticism which few audiences could ignore. By comparison, travelling horn soloists suddenly seemed unexciting, and the solos and chamber music for wind and horns which had appeared regularly in concerts in the Classical period suddenly disappeared almost completely from concert programmes in the 1830s. Indeed, the only place where audiences might hear a work for solo horn in London after the middle of the century was as a novelty in the deliberately populist concerts which were run by entrepreneurs such as Louis Jullien.

Chamber music: nineteenth century

The first wind quintets were composed early in the nineteenth century by Antoine Reicha to exploit the brilliant playing of musicians associated with the Paris Conservatoire. One of the earliest was played at the Conservatoire on 14 April 1814 with Louis Colin on the horn,[35] but most of the quintets' horn parts were written for Reicha's composition pupil, Louis Dauprat. Other composers who then tried their hand at the form included Franz Danzi in Karlsruhe, but in publishing his 3 Quintets, op. 56, in 1821, Danzi seems to have recognised that the main market for such works was in France, for he forsook his normal German publisher in favour of the Parisian Maurice Schlesinger and allowed their dedication to Reicha to appear in larger letters than his own name on the title page.

Sonatas for horn and piano had been unknown in the eighteenth century, when the instruments' radically different sonorities and characteristics were very difficult to match. The contemporary horn had a gentler sound than today's instrument, but even the loudest eighteenth-century fortepiano was substantially quieter than a modern concert grand, and was endowed with far less sustaining power. Beethoven was the first composer to feel confident with the two instruments, writing his Sonata op. 17 to play with Giovanni Punto in 1800, but Danzi, Krufft, F.E. Thurner and Ries followed suit and, as pianos became louder, works for horn and piano became more common. In the 1830s and 1840s composers associated with Vienna suddenly produced a flurry of songs with horn and piano accompaniment and in the early years of the nineteenth century, Paris attracted a large number of works for horn and harp, but few of these have survived in the mainstream repertoire.

Valve horns versus hand horns

France

Although Sporck first heard horns played at Versailles, the spotlight did not return to France until the end of the eighteenth century, when a music school for the National Guard emerged from the apparently unpropitious circumstances of the French Revolution. In 1795 the school metamorphosed into the Paris Conservatoire, and its opening to 351 pupils and 115 teachers in 1796 marked the beginning of an institution which was to have a very considerable effect on standards of horn playing and teaching across Europe. Its main impact, however, was inevitably in France, for although the Bohemian tradition was represented in the teaching of Heinrich Domnich, the work of Frédéric Duvernoy, Louis Dauprat and Jacques-François Gallay ensured the development of a distinctively French school of playing which was only marginally influenced by the invention of the valve horn.

The most characteristic feature of horn playing at the Paris Conservatoire was the professors' conscientiously pursued objection to valve horns and their music. The main problem, in their minds, lay in valves' capacity to even out tone colour, and while similar arguments raged in Germany without greatly inhibiting the spread of valve horns, in France the new instrument was largely ostracised until the end of the century. The doyen of French teachers, Louis Dauprat, acquired a valve horn in 1827, but soon abandoned any thought of using it, commenting that with valves the instrument 'would lose its character and the true qualities of its natural and stopped sounds. Most of these latter have a charm that is particularly theirs and which serve, so to speak, as shadings and nuances which contrast with the natural sounds. It must then be presumed that, far from gaining by their complete removal, the horn would lose a great deal.'[36] Pierre-Joseph Meifred introduced the valve horn to the Paris Conservatoire in a concert in 1828, and was allowed to run a valve horn class there from 1833, but his isolation was emphasised in 1842 when Dauprat was replaced by his former pupil, the brilliant hand horn player Jacques-François Gallay.

Meifred's thinking was, however, both conciliatory and reasonable, and he explained in his tutor that he saw the valve horn not as a replacement for the hand horn but as a new and different instrument which had particular uses in the middle and lower ranges. As abandoning hand stopping would mean the loss of the 'special character' which gives the horn 'indefinable charm',[37] he suggests ways of playing stopped notes on the valve horn, a practice which Berlioz requires in, for example, the *Symphonie Fantastique*, 5th movement, bar 9, where the 3rd horn solo is marked 'bouché avec les cylindres' ('stopped with the valves'). Finally, Meifred wanted composers to have the opportunity to understand the potential of the new instrument, and must have felt that there was hope when Gounod's *Six Mélodies* for valve horn and piano (*c.* 1840) were followed in about 1854 by Saint-Saëns' 'Andante' for valve horn and organ. His retirement in 1864, however, came at about the same time as Gallay's death, and instead of filling both posts, the Conservatoire combined them under Jean Mohr, a dedicated hand horn player whose tutor, dated 1871,[38] reflected Parisian opinion by completely ignoring the existence of valve horns.

French players were, however, less united in their opinion of cor mixte, an early nineteenth-century hand horn technique in which players specialised in middle register work, ignoring where possible the highest and lowest notes and transposing all parts onto the F, E, Eb and D crooks. The main proponent of the style was Frédéric Duvernoy, a player of 'great security and power'[39] who, until 1816, was senior professor of the horn at the Conservatoire. It was also adopted by Punto's pupil, Luigi Belloli, who, as first horn at La Scala, Milan, was the leading Italian player in the early years of the century, and whose concertos demonstrate the high degree of hand stopping and the narrow range which are typical of the style.

Belloli's pupil, Giovanni Puzzi, veered between cor basse and cor mixte playing, but although the only important work in the style is the *Prélude, Thème et Variations* ('Péchés de Vieillesse, vol. 9'), which Rossini wrote for Eugène Vivier in 1857, Domnich regarded cor mixte as a major threat to the long-standing distinction between cor alto players and their lower, cor basse colleagues. While Duvernoy recognised his colleagues' strength of feeling, tactfully omitting any reference to cor mixte in his tutor, and advising that students should continue to train as high or low players, Domnich makes no secret of his hostility, describing it as a 'disastrous development which has been introduced into almost all our orchestras'. Hitherto, 'several years of unrelenting study and work' had been needed to learn 'purity of tone and accuracy of pitch in the two extremes of the instrument'. Now, 'deprived equally of high and of low tones, the cors mixtes . . . are able to play neither on the C crook, nor on those of A and B♭. How do they manage? When they are given a piece in B♭, instead of being provided with the proper instruments in this key, the horn in E♭ is employed. They make use of the horn in D if the piece is in A, and if it is in C it is necessary to use the horn in F.' A composer who has written in one of these keys for conventional hand horn technique and hopes to express 'the noise of war, the glory of victory, or the pomp of triumph, arranges the horns in such a manner that they do it all without the aid of the hand in the bell. But as cors mixtes are obliged to transpose, . . . the sonorous notes often become stopped notes and brilliant sounds become dark and lugubrious accents. Furthermore, in the factitious scale which results from the transposition, the artist must at times change the second part by playing notes absolutely destitute of tone, and which can be played only as a dull quivering'.[40] Although cor mixte playing itself died out quite quickly it contributed to the longevity of the hand horn in France, partly because its exponents were so skilled at hand stopping, and partly because it fuelled the Paris Conservatoire's intransigence in the face of change.

Outside the Conservatoire, opinion gradually began to change. 'The prejudice against the cor à pistons is so deep rooted that the most skilful artists have disdained this instrument', wrote F.J. Fétis in 1865. 'They are convinced that the tone of the cor à pistons is inferior to that of the hand horn, but, if some men of talent such as Mohr, Pacquis and Baneux would study it, they would soon have proof that their quality of tone had not lost any of its purity . . . The resistance, moreover against the adoption of the cor à pistons in the orchestra in Paris and in the provinces of France seems plain nonsense to me.'[41] Further pressure came from composers, for the popularity of Wagner's operas left Parisian players no alternative but to use valves and when French composers such as Halévy, Meyerbeer and Massenet started to write for the instrument the Conservatoire's position was increasingly isolated. César Franck's decision to include four valve horns in his Symphony (1886–8) acted as another nail in its philosophical coffin and, in 1898, Jean Mohr's successor, the devoted hand horn player François Brémond, bowed to the inevitable by organising an informal weekly valve horn class. Five years later, he ended the country's official opposition to valves by decreeing that the test pieces in the Conservatoire's annual competition must from now on be played on the valve horn,[42] but a further French quirk, the ascending third valve, survived well into the twentieth century, and is described in chapter 3.

Germany

Although German players were relatively quick to adopt horns with three rotary valves for orchestral work, they did not do so without some regret, and while Borsdorf recalled that hand horns were still used in Dresden's Catholic church when he studied in the city in 1879,[43] Brahms wrote almost all of his horn parts for the natural instrument. Joseph Lewy insisted in 1850 that hand stopping should be regarded as an essential component of valve horn technique,[44] and Franz Ludwig Schubert made the same point in 1865 after 'censuring' conductors for tolerating 'the use of valved horns pitched in F to replace all possible crookings of the natural horns'.[45] Friedrich Gumbert voiced a similar opinion in 1879: 'If one has a dull, rough and fuzzy tone on the valve horn, one will do no better on the natural horn . . . If one desires a colourful, mixed effect, in which stopped sounds can be advantageous, like the mutes of string instruments, so then the valves on the horn are no hindrance, because one can make just as much use of the hand on the valve horn as on the natural horn.' He added, however, that Jean Désiré Artôt, professor of horn at the Conservatory in Brussels, and Adolf Lindner, the first horn at Leipzig's Gewandhaus from 1854, managed to retain 'the precious quality of their [hand horn] tone' when they played the valve horn.[46] Wagner, too, found that some players – who probably included Joseph Lewy – had learned to overcome the 'undeniable loss in beauty of tone' which had followed the introduction of valves,[47] and was therefore happy to reserve stopped notes for special effects while relying mainly on the use of the valves.

Adam Wirth, the head of horn teaching at the Royal Musical Institute in Würzburg, felt differently, asserting in 1877 that 'the piston horn has arrived at a state of perfection in respect of its range as well as the equality of its sounds'. However,

> it is often abused. This instrument is frequently used in a way contrary to its character, as much by composers as by conductors who

arrange scores. The [natural] horn was one of the most excellent singing instruments . . . and at the same time, one of the instruments most able to produce superb effects in the orchestra when used properly . . . You hear so often . . . that the horn has lost something of the beauty of its sound as a result of the mechanism which it has adopted, that you would sometimes think that it must sound like a trumpet or a trombone. The problem is not the instrument's sound, but the distorted way in which it is used. It is fair to say that the more simple the horn line, the better its sound.' [48]

Nonetheless, Wirth advises students to start on the natural horn before learning to use valves, an idea which Carl Klotz had suggested in 1863 would give beginners a chance to acquire 'that beautiful and mellow tone so peculiar to the simple instrument' rather than the 'noisy, quavering and rough tone which is so common among players of the chromatic horn'.[49]

England

English players trod a middle way in the dispute between hand and valve horns, for until late in the nineteenth century many preferred to use a two-valved instrument. The brass band instruments which burst onto the English market in the middle of the century were invariably equipped with three valves, but Algernon Rose[50] suggests that the eventual success of horns with valves had much to do with military needs: 'in the army a valve horn was found preferable by many bandmasters to no horn, because properly arranged horn parts do much to make a military band sound well, and the difficulties of the simple horn used to take as many years to master as the present duration of a soldier's service'. That there was still some support for the hand horn outside the army, however, is demonstrated by the publication in London in 1880 of the 'Grand Method', a volume which combined the content of the tutors by Dauprat, Gallay and Meifred. [51] Meifred was writing for the valve horn, but overall the combined tutor is hostile to valves which, 'being constantly used will destroy the peculiarity of the tone of the French Horn and reduce it to the rank of an ordinary saxhorn'. The three-valved instrument was gradually gaining ground, however, and its progress was probably helped by the arrival of the renowned German player, Adolf Borsdorf, in London in 1879 and then, three years later, by his compatriot, Franz Paersch, who was destined for Buxton and then the Hallé Orchestra.

Although Borsdorf's arrival is often seen as a major event in the history of horn playing in Britain, he was, in fact, only one of a number of continental players who worked in London during the nineteenth century. The demise of the travelling horn player and of the privately retained orchestras which were a feature of eighteenth-century Europe left many players looking for alternative employment, and although the development in London of a class of freelance professional musicians was a rather anonymous alternative to the international acclaim which had been accorded to Punto, Türrschmidt and Palsa, it clearly had attractions for foreign musicians. Players named Steglich and Eckhoff played in the orchestra of the Philharmonic Society, and by the mid-nineteenth century Dauprat's pupil, Antoine Pacquis, was active in the capital, earning a reputation as 'the last of the great hand horn players in this country.' He was also the English agent for Raoux and may have been working in this capacity when he gave a demonstration of the valve horn in London in 1862, for he was far from at home on the instrument. A member of the Hallé Orchestra between 1871 and 1874, he 'tried in vain' to play Wagner's horn parts on the hand horn, and according to Borsdorf, eventually, 'threw the music on the floor and danced on it. Hallé tried to calm him down, but he merely exclaimed, "I do not care. Zat is not the way to write for the instrument", and executed another war dance'.[52] On 27 January 1872, another foreign player, Fritz Wendland, made a highly unusual solo appearance at Crystal Palace,[53] where he played a Notturno for horn and orchestra by Carl Reinecke, and this led to his appointment both as first horn in the Philharmonic Society and in Mann's Crystal Palace Orchestra. The arrival of Adolf Borsdorf from Saxony to play in the stage band at Covent Garden was certainly to have a significant effect on English horn playing, but, seen in context, it was not the bolt from the blue which is often depicted.

It cannot have been easy for English horn players to understand what attracted their continental colleagues to London, for in the mid-nineteenth century life as a horn player in the capital could be hard. Two of their number – Giovanni Puzzi and Henry Jarrett – died wealthy, but they made their money from their work as impresarios, not as horn players. As far as the others were concerned, there was enough work available to enable a handful of players to survive as long as they kept on working, but stopping meant almost certain disaster. The archives of the Royal Society of Musicians are full of human catastrophe: John Rae, for example, suffered an ulcerated neck in 1834 and struggled to play for a further two years although his salary of 10s per week was insufficient to support his wife and four children.[54] Retirement was equally catastrophic: Rae's brother James was described in 1830 as 'one of the best concert players in the kingdom' [55] and was praised for his 'extremely mellow and sweet tone' but left the Philharmonic Concerts at the end of 1858 after thirty-two years, and two years later was dismissed from the Italian Opera after thirty-five years' service. His petition to the RSM 'cited slackness of trade' as the cause of his problems, and after his death his wife suffered twenty-three years of destitution.[56] A possible reason for such poverty was identified in the *Illustrated London News* in 1850: in connection with a forthcoming benefit concert for Henry Platt, who had lost his teeth after playing at the highest level throughout his career, the paper wrote, 'Performers on the horn, although expected to be first-rate artists, obtain very few pupils, and the scale of remuneration is too small to make a provision for the future, in order to be prepared for such a calamity as has closed the career of one of the most celebrated players this country has produced.'[57]

The absence of teaching opportunities was genuine enough: the Royal Academy of Music had opened in 1822, and Platt was appointed professor four years later, but the only regular horn students in the early days were William Daniel and J.F. Hopgood,[58] for Charles Harper studied privately with Puzzi.[59] Instead, would-be professional players often came, like Platt and the Raes, from military backgrounds or, like Harper, Charles Catchpole and Thomas Mann, from established families of musicians.[60]

Bohemia

Players in Prague seem to have had no concerns about moving to valved horns at an early date. Joseph Kail, the first horn in Prague's National Theatre from 1826, had experience of helping both Riedl and Uhlmann in their experiments with valves in Vienna, and soon began to teach valve trumpet and trombone at the Prague Conservatoire.[61] Two songs with valve horn obbligato by František Škroup date from about 1840 and were published in Prague as his op. 6 and op. 15; both are printed for horn in E♭, and as both have a key signature it is likely that the publisher expected them to be played on the valve horn. 'Liebes Thal', op. 15 would, however, work easily on the natural horn if it were transposed from concert D♭ to E♭ and so may have been composed for a valveless instrument.

Russia

Germany was also the main influence on Russian music in the second half of the nineteenth century. Friedrich Homilius, the first horn at St Petersburg's Imperial Theatre, had previously played in a military band in Dresden[62] and was also among the teaching staff when the St Petersburg Conservatoire was founded in 1862. Glinka's horn writing is clearly intended for hand horns, but later composers' horn parts are modelled on contemporary German writing and were probably played on instruments which were pitched in F with rotary valves along German lines.

Italy

The Danish horn player and diplomat, Rudoph Bay,[63] recorded his pleasure at hearing the hand horn played by Antonio Tosoroni in Livorno in February 1822: 'Never have I heard such virtuosity as his. His masterly treatment of this instrument was like a flute.' The earliest Italian valve horns were probably manufactured in the same year, however – an instrument by Lorenzo dall'Asta, but with valves rather like Uhlmann's, is said to be preserved in Bologna's Museo Civico Mediavale [64] – and although Tosoroni took to them with alacrity, Bay was dismayed at the change when he heard him play again twenty years later. Tosoroni was now employed at the Grand Ducal Chapel at Florence, and his brilliant technique allowed him to play a violin concerto on the horn, yet, 'it was no longer those soft melting sounds from the past in Livorno; his horn, by God, had become a valve horn, and his mouthpiece, formerly the size of a thimble, through which he squeezed the highest notes like a nightingale, had now turned into a clumsy kettle, growling bass notes like a bear'.

Tosoroni is said to have published the first Italian valve horn method, *Metodo per Corno a 3 pistoni*,[65] at about the time of his second meeting with Bay, but others were less whole-hearted in their adoption of valves: Raniero Cacciamani's *Metodo d'Istruzione par Corno da Caccia*,[66] which followed in 1860, introduces exercises for the natural horn before progressing to the

Example 2.1 Verdi: Otello Act One, Miniature Score p. 94 (IMC edition).

Horn 1 in E

valve horn and Renato Meucci says that as late as 1881 some Italian musicians hesitated to 'abandon completely the old instrument in favour of the new one; some of them felt that, in teaching, the practice of the one model should be alternated with that of the other'.[67] Something of this attachment to hand horn technique is clear even in Verdi's 'Otello' (1887), for, apart from the opening grace notes, the passage shown in example 2.1 would have been regarded as exemplary hand horn writing by players of Dauprat's era. Even the low D and Db are approached stylistically, downwards and by step.

3   Equipment

Despite the apparent complexity of the modern horn, its design – a mouth-piece entering a coiled, part cylindrical, part conical brass tube which culminates in a rapidly flaring bell – is the same now as it has ever been. Similarly, the essential principles of playing it – the use of lips, tongue and lungs to control the basic elements of pitch, attack, timbre and volume – are the same today as when it was taking its first steps as a member of the orchestra. Nevertheless, as composers', performers' and listeners' expectations and perceptions have shifted during the last 350 years, a number of significant changes in instrumental design have taken place. Visually, the most dramatic of these was the addition of valves, but others have also played a major part in defining the horn's rôle through the ages.

Development of the horn

Earliest instruments; cor de chasse

The technology necessary to work and solder brass has been applied to musical instruments since the Middle Ages, but the first instruments which are recognisable as horns appeared during the seventeenth century. Their precise design was variable – some seem to have been very tightly coiled, while others consisted of a single wide hoop – but whatever their shape the surviving repertoire is tiny.[1] The traditional French cor de chasse, which was formed as either a single or a double coil, was probably invented around 1680, and was designed to be played on horseback during Louis XIV's hunting parties, but moved into the concert hall almost immediately.

Master crook and coupler system

With their fixed mouthpipe, absence of tuning slide, and unalter-able length, however, these horns raised very real problems in concert performance. A different instrument was needed for each key, and while the pragmatist might have hoped to get away with owning instruments in the most common keys of D and F, they could not be finely tuned, and the alternative of getting the group to tune to the horn was clearly unsatisfactory. By as early as 1700[2] the Leichnamschneider brothers in Vienna had begun to manufacture instruments equipped with a tapered master crook – into which the mouthpiece fitted – and a series of one or more cylindrical couplers which were then inserted between the master crook and the horn. These allowed a player to own a single instrument and to 'crook' it into all the common keys, fine tuning by fitting short pieces of tubing – 'tuning bits' – between the mouthpiece and the master crook. This, the master crook and coupler system, was popular by the later part of the eighteenth century and in England lasted well into the nineteenth.

A detailed account of how to add couplers to each other appears in Charles Tully's *Tutor for the French Horn*[3] which was published in London in about 1840:

> Some horns have five [coupler] crooks, and others have all master-crooks, namely a crook for every key, as marked at the end which receives the mouthpiece. We recommend the learner to provide himself with a five crook horn . . . There is besides an extra small crook . . . to put the horn in A; and a still smaller crook or tube to put it into B♭-alto.

This works well for parts requiring middle register crooks, but in high keys the body of the instrument is very close to the player's face, and when all the couplers are inserted for low keys it is so far away that the instrument can start to wobble, with inevitable consequences for accuracy.

Inventionshorn/cor solo; tuning slide

Clearly the same problems afflicted eighteenth-century players, and Anton Hampel's 'Inventionshorn' improved matters considerably. First manufactured by the Dresden maker Johann Werner around 1750, this involved cutting one of the instrument's hoops, bending the two cut ends so that they were parallel with each other and then adding the crook to the two legs of tubing. The process of adding the crooks to the body of the horn, while leaving the mouthpipe fixed, solved most of the problems associated with the master crook and coupler system, but lack of space meant that it

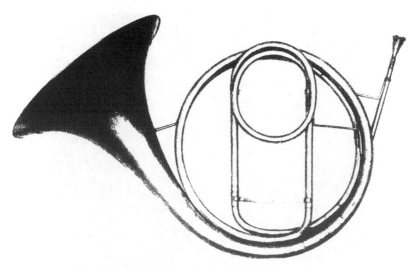

1 Inventionshorn by F. Korn, Mainz, *c.* 1825–30

was now difficult – though not impossible – to design an instrument which could accept both the longest and the shortest crooks. The Inventionshorn also suffered from the lack of any tuning device until around 1776, when J.G. Haltenhof introduced a slide to replace the tenon and socket fitting.[4] About four years later, the brilliant Parisian manufacturers Joseph and Lucien-Joseph Raoux refined it further by deciding that just five crooks were needed, and, working in association with Türrschmidt, supplied their 'Cor solo' with body crooks in G, F, E, E♭ and D. This instrument was suitable only for soloists, for orchestral players needed to be able to play in other keys, but as soloists played almost exclusively in F, E, E♭ and D – the most effective keys for hand stopping – the G crook seems strangely superfluous.

Terminal crooks

An extremely popular compromise between the Inventionshorn and the coupler system was invented in France around 1800 and involved the manufacture of terminal crooks for each key. These instruments kept the distance between the mouthpiece and the body of the horn fairly constant, and avoided wobble by having only one joint which was reliant on friction. Players usually owned separate crooks for B♭ alto, A, G, F, E, E♭, D and C. From about 1828 the set might also include one in A♭ alto,[5] and low B and B♭ crooks were made occasionally, but it was usual to reach these keys by adding

2 Orchestral horn by Halary, Paris *c.* 1830. Shown here with a D crook.

couplers to the C crook. The main drawback to this system was the quantity of brass tubing which the player had to carry around, usually in a large rectangular box which had slots for the horn itself as well as for each crook. Although the boxes were bulky, they were often works of art in themselves.

Characteristics of crooks

The discovery of crooks is usually a great and unexpected pleasure to performers who have previously used only modern double horns, for they differ greatly in timbre and response. The highest keys, B♭ and A, are very focused and penetrating in tone, and respond quickly, making rapid tonguing easy, but they soon become tiring to play because they are usually used for very high parts. At the opposite end of the spectrum, the low B♭ and C

crooks have a rich, dark, almost muddy tone, but, because of their length –
B♭ has 18 feet (about 5.5m) of tubing – are slow to speak. Indeed, the
difference in response between a horn crooked in B♭ alto and one in B♭ basso
is akin to the difference in handling between a sports car and a lorry. Even
the four 'soloist's' crooks – F, E, E♭ and D – which together provide the best
compromise between brilliance and mellowness of tone, feel quite different
from each other.

Changes of bore

The term 'bore' is often used rather loosely to refer to the size of the
lead pipe and bell throat, but the size of the tubing in the middle of the
instrument also has an effect on its sound. Vienna horns, for example, are
generally considered to be wide bore instruments because of the size of their
bell throat, but at 10.5–11 mm their middle tubing is among the narrowest
of any modern instrument. Similarly, many modern players think of horns
by Alexander as having a medium bore, but their middle tubing is very wide.

In very general terms, the bell size has increased as orchestras have
become louder, and as a result, a modern, 'large-bore' horn looks monstrous
by comparison with its Baroque predecessor. It was, however, not volume
but the invention of hand-stopping which made it necessary to enlarge the
bell throat during the eighteenth century, for it was not usually possible to
insert enough of the hand into the bell of a Baroque horn either to make a
quality sound or to be comfortable. The ideal bell throat, therefore, was big
enough to accept the player's hand, but no bigger than was needed to stop
the note with the smallest possible movement of the palm. If the throat
became too wide, the quality of the stopped notes was reduced because the
hand had to move further to correct their intonation. It is therefore not
practical to try to learn to play the hand horn on a modern wide-throated
double horn. In any case, composers today write stopped notes when they
want a different sound from the horn's open notes; in the eighteenth and
nineteenth centuries accomplished players aimed to make the stopped notes
sound more like open ones, although complete equality was neither possible
nor desirable.

The invention of the valve

In 1815, Heinrich Stölzel, a horn player from the Court of Pless in
Upper Silesia, performed in Berlin on a horn which exploited his invention

of the valve during the previous year.[6] Unfortunately, as this instrument has not survived we do not know what it looked like, but we do know that it had two valves and was built by Griessling and Schlott. Stölzel then teamed up with Friedrich Blühmel, a musician whose title, 'Berg-Hoboist', seems to have meant that he played in a works or mine band, and in 1818 they patented the invention. In retrospect, this was one of the most important turning points in the history of brass instruments, and yet players and manufacturers were surprisingly slow to take it up.

Stölzel and Blühmel were, however, not the first to try to make the horn fully chromatic, and if other people had not improved on their design it might have fallen by the wayside along with, for example, Charles Clagget's Chromatic Trumpet and the associated Chromatic French Horn. Patented in 1788 this was, in essence, two horns with a common mouthpiece and a primitive valve operated by a lever. Said by its inventor to play a complete chromatic scale, the instrument is described in detail in Morley-Pegge,[7] and was played by Mortellari 'in the Presence of many Amateurs and Professors of Music of the first Class', in a performance of an anonymous Divertimento for horn solo[8] at Hanover Square on 18 May 1790. Having found the instrument very easy to learn, Mortellari also played some 'airs' of his own, but neither these nor the Divertimento contain anything which would trouble an experienced hand horn player, and after causing mild interest the Chromatic Trumpet and French Horn were forgotten.

Blühmel and Stölzel soon went their separate ways and Stölzel altered his design from 'square' or 'box' valves to a tubular shape. The Parisian makers, Halary and Labbaye, then made some further improvements to the design, and Labbaye began to build valve horns in collaboration with Pierre-Joseph Meifred. One valve lowered the pitch of the instrument by a tone, the second by a semitone, and when in 1819 the Leipzig manufacturer C.F. Sattler[9] introduced a third valve to lower the pitch by a tone and a half, the horn was fully chromatic for the first time.

'Stölzel' valves are easily identifiable because the bottom of the valve forms one of its windways. They lingered on through the nineteenth century, and could still be found on cheap cornets up to the beginning of the first world war,[10] but an alternative, Leopold Uhlmann's Vienna valves, was patented as early as 1830.[11] Characterised by long rods which connect the fingerplates to the far end of the valves, these also enjoyed some popularity

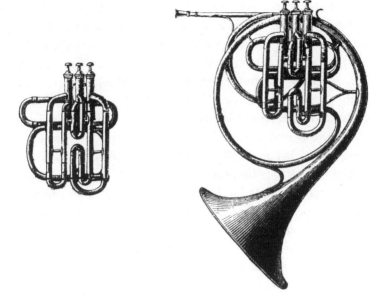

3 Horn with 3 Périnet valves and sauterelle (detachable valve section).
Illustration taken from 1898 catalogue for *L'Association Générale des
Ouvriers.*

outside Vienna, and were sometimes used on horns built in Belgium and
Markneukirchen. The mechanism itself can be slow to operate, but a picture
of a horn with valves of this type appears in Nemetz's tutor of 1829. [12] Joseph
Riedl, who also worked in Vienna, followed with the rotary valve in 1835[13]
and a fourth design, by François Périnet, with both windways in the side of
the casing, followed in 1839.[14] This was used on instruments which were
built along French lines, such as those made by Hawkes and by Besson, and
although horn players today regard them as old fashioned, Périnet, or
'piston', valves are still used on trumpets.

Omnitonic horns

Players' ambivalence about the development of valves naturally led
makers to experiment with alternatives which might combine chromatic
flexibility with the tonal responsiveness of the hand horn. One possibility

seemed to be to incorporate a complete set of crooks in a single instrument, and then to design a mechanism which would enable the player to change between them very quickly. Some of these so-called 'omnitonic' horns were quite impractical in terms of their appearance and weight, but the 'Radius French Horn' which the London player John Callcott designed and displayed at the Great Exhibition of 1851 received flattering testimonials from the city's leading performers, including Giovanni Puzzi, Charles Harper, Henry Hardy and Hermann Steglich. Their opinion is substantiated by the only known surviving model, for since its restoration, the Bate Collection's elegant Callcott horn has proved itself eminently playable.

Although the omnitonic horn was never adopted on a large scale, it is important because it was probably the instrument on which Saint-Saëns' major repertoire piece, the 'Morceau de Concert', op. 94 was first performed. Composed in 1887, this was the second work which Saint-Saëns had written for Henri Chaussier, but while the 'Romance', op. 67, was clearly for hand horn, the 'Morceau de Concert' requires a more chromatic instrument. Chaussier was a pupil of Jean Mohr at the Conservatoire, and as a dedicated hand horn player is said to have had so much difficulty adapting to the valve horn when he worked for a season in Berlin that he developed his own omnitonic horn, publishing a description of it in 1889.[15] The surviving diagrams show that the left hand operated three Périnet valves and a thumb valve to change its crooks, but its fingering was so idiosyncratic that it had no real chance of success at this relatively late date. Whether it made any noticeable difference to Chaussier's playing is not known: although he was a fine soloist with a spectacular top register, his orchestral playing was so bad that Brémond said, 'if I was conductor of the Clowns' Orchestra I wouldn't want him as 2nd horn'.[16]

The double horn

Dauprat explains[17] that his teacher Joseph Kenn, gave more 'charm' to hand horn performances of one of Rosetti's double concertos by using a high A crook to play high-lying passages which had been written for the E crook. This idea gained ground and as the century wore on, it became more common for players with terminally crooked valve horns to make high passages more secure by replacing the F crook with a shorter one. In southern

Germany, players such as Franz Strauss preferred to use a B♭ crook, while in England A was the norm. This was often at the expense of intonation and tone quality – Reinecke and von Bülow refused to allow their orchestral players this option[18] – but increasingly difficult horn parts forced shorter crooks onto many players, and in 1898 the *Deutsche Musiker Zeitung*[19] was the scene of much debate on the merits of the practice. While the controversy raged, Eduard Kruspe began work on a compromise, and in the same journal advertised the 'System Gumpert-Kruspe', the first double horn.

The Gumpert-Kruspe instrument was, its maker claimed,

> a new design of horn which should be brought to the attention of all parties, a product of many years of thought and tireless experiments by the Court Musician Edmund Gumpert of Meiningen and the Court Instrument maker Eduard Kruspe at Erfurt. The basis of this invention is an F horn: simply by using the thumb to change the direction of a [pair of] rotary valves, the performer may shut off the F crook and its valve slides, causing the air column to pass through the B♭ crook and B♭ valve slides. These are combined in the most ingenious manner and allow an immediate ascent to the highest notes of the B♭ horn, from the full-toned F horn.[20]

In fact, Kruspe's first model was a compensating instrument whose longer, front rank of valve slides in B♭ could be joined, via a pair of valves operated by the thumb, to a shorter rank of slides so that together they put the horn into F. The Viennese manufacturer, Uhlmann, had tried a similar idea around 1870,[21] but it had not caught on, and indeed Kruspe's first attempt at a thumb valve proved less easy to operate than the advertisement suggested. However, he replaced it with a single rotary valve in 1900, and in the same year the Berlin maker C.F. Schmidt produced the first real full double horn, with the B♭ and F sides having only the mouthpipe and the bell in common. This earned a considerable following in the United States of America, especially around Chicago, but while the piston valve which operated the F/B♭ change was easy to depress, it proved tiring to hold down for long periods, and was very difficult to release in a hurry. Alexander of Mainz built their first double horn in 1906,[22] and the full double design which Kruspe first built in 1902 is still in use today.

Regional preferences

France

In France, players valued the range of sounds associated with stopped notes, and had no intention of abandoning hand stopping. 'The too frequent use of the pistons would in itself', wrote Gounod,[23] 'deprive the horn of that pure and melancholy colour which is natural to it', and few of his compatriots changed to valves at all. For those who did, two seemed quite sufficient, and weighed less than three – a consideration for players who usually also had a full set of detachable crooks to carry around. Even Meifred at first preferred two to three and, before he discovered the attractions of an ascending third valve, is reported to have said that 'if he could do all that was asked with one valve, then he'd make do with only one'.[24] By the end of the century, the battle was largely won and three-valved horns clearly represented the way for the future, but a very late reference to two-valved horns occurs in the 1898 catalogue of L'Association Générale des Ouvriers,[25] which offers in its standard range a natural horn, a two-valved model, and one for three valves. Its 'Cors 1er choix', however, include a hand horn, a three valve horn, and – most expensively – a three-valved 'artist's special model', suggesting that by now two-valved horns would not be the choice of the experienced professional.

Ascending third valve

The ascending third valve is unique to France, where it was invented in 1847[26] by Jules Halary and immediately adopted by Meifred. Whereas players elsewhere invariably use a descending third valve to lower the pitch of their instrument by a tone and a half, many French players believed that 'great advantages in accuracy of pitch and sureness of emission'[27] were derived from a third valve which raised the pitch of the instrument by a tone. The device has been used by a number of leading performers from Meifred to Georges Barboteu, and while Brémond himself owned a Raoux with Besson valves,[28] he collaborated with the manufacturers Schoenaers-Millereau to design a horn whose third valve could be ascending or descending at will. The ascending system was so popular during the twentieth century that until recently Selmer built a double horn with three piston

4 Horn with 2 Stölzel valves. Illustration taken from the cover of the
English translation of Charles Gounod's *Méthode de Cor à pistons.*

valves and a rotary F/B♭ change as their rival to the all-conquering German
rotary valve double horn.

Italy

An interesting problem arises in nineteenth-century Italian opera
scores, for from about 1830 onwards composers appeared to require their
players to use A, A♭ and G basso crooks, which in theory did not exist. These
could be obtained by adding several couplers to the C crook, but it is very
difficult to make the air move in the longest crooks, and, at such a low pitch,
hand stopped notes are difficult to tune. The highly skilled hand horn
players of the 1830s–1840s may, of course, have been relatively confident in
such a low tessitura, but they must still have found it difficult to play the

Example 3.1 Donizetti: Don Pasquale (1843), bars 23–31. (Ricordi edition).

Horn 1 in C

fairly chromatic 3rd and 4th horn parts in Bellini's *Norma* and in *Lucia di Lammermoor* (1835) and *Don Pasquale* (1843) by Donizetti (see Example 3.1). Italian composers may have written in this way to give players a choice between hand and valve horns, or their notation may simply have reflected a local convention, but it is also possible that some players coped with such parts by resorting to Giuseppe Pelitti's omnitonic horn.[29] This had only a short life, but when it was invented in 1845 it was capable of playing 'closed and open' notes in most keys, and ten years later it was refined 'to give the horn any desired pitch'.

Vienna

While the fanatical hand horn players of Paris fought to hold their ground in the face of valves, the Viennese market for hand horns remained sufficiently strong for Uhlmann to continue making them until around the turn of the century. From as early as 1835,[30] however, Johann Strauss Snr's orchestra was using Vienna horns, instruments which were pitched predominantly in F but had detachable crooks and Vienna valves, and in 1883, [31] Josef Schantl founded the Wiener Waldhorn Verein to preserve and promulgate their sound. Very few changes have been made to the instrument since, and while its advocates point to its full tone, thrilling forte sound and its capacity for smooth legatos, its detractors criticise its vulnerability to split notes in the upper register and the relative lack of agility which results from its slow-moving valve mechanism.

England

Valve horns were first manufactured in England by Pace in 1830[32] and the hand horn/valve horn debate began to be resolved around the middle of the nineteenth century. By 1897, afficionados of the hand horn were to be found only 'occasionally',[33] and although an early twentieth-century catalogue from Jérôme Thibouville-Lamy[34] offers natural horns with ten crooks at £3 16s 0d as well as three-valved instruments with five and ten crooks, the market can only have been small.

There was less agreement, however, about the ideal number of valves, and in some circles the two-valved horn was still seen as the norm even at the start of the twentieth century. An undated photograph shows Borsdorf aged about thirty holding a three-valved horn with the Périnet valves[35] which were the usual choice for such instruments, but Blandford[36] recalled that Robert Keevil, 'an excellent cor basse of the old school', attached a set of three rotary valves to his Raoux. Stölzel valves were more common on two-valved horns, and a picture of such an instrument was included on the cover of the English edition of Gounod's tutor, which was still on sale in 1890.[37] Lafleur's tutor, which was published around 1880,[38] had individual sections on two- and three-valved horns, and although a pamphlet published by Weekes & Co in 1883[39] does not specify the type of instrument being used, the instructions on playing are clearly for an instrument with two valves. The 1900 edition of Grove's Dictionary[40] includes a line-drawing of a two-valved horn, but in the 1910 edition this was replaced by one with three valves.[41]

Germany; the Czech border villages

No single German city rivalled Paris's domination of French horn playing in the nineteenth century, and equally important players and manufacturers could be found in Munich, Berlin, Leipzig, Dresden and Hamburg. Nuremberg had dominated the manufacture of German horns during the Baroque, but its influence was waning by the late eighteenth century and, in its place, the neighbouring Czech border villages of Markneukirchen, Klingenthal and Graslitz (today, Kraslice in the Czech Republic) were assuming an importance in brass-instrument making which was out of all proportion to their size. Manufacturing started in the area in 1755, when

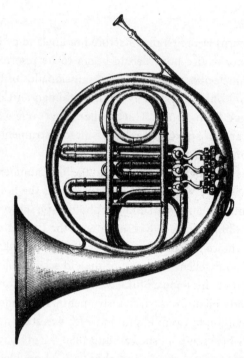

5 Typical, German-style, nineteenth-century rotary-valved horn with fixed mouthpipe. Illustration taken from Hugo Riemann's *Catechism of Musical Instruments* (1888).

Isaak Eschenbach, a native of Markneukirchen, established a business building horns there after learning his trade in Leipzig, some sixty miles away.[42] Graslitz had a famous brass foundry in 1786, and by 1871 the copper-rich Erzegebirge Mountains had proved so fruitful that makers in the Markneukirchen area turned out 20,000 brass instruments per year, half of the total made in the whole of Germany.[43] Part of their success may also have been due to their flexibility: rather than specialise in a single design of horn, the makers of Markneukirchen supplied players from a wide range of backgrounds, building horns in a variety of designs, and not restricting themselves to the rotary valves which were the norm in nineteenth-century Germany. The Graslitz makers also had access to the Bohemian market, for Prague was only one hundred miles away.[44]

The design of valve horns gradually changed as they became more popular, and once they were no longer constrained by the requirements of hand stopping, the size of their bell throat began to increase. Austro-Bohemian hand horns had always tended to have a bigger bell throat than instruments manufactured in France, but George Bernard Shaw thought that he detected a substantial difference in tone colour in 1892, when Covent Garden brought in some German players for a performance of *Siegfried* which Mahler was to conduct.[45] 'Instead of three distinct and finely contrasted families of thoroughbred trombones, horns and tubas', he wrote, 'we had a huge tribe of mongrels, differing chiefly in size. I felt that some ancestor of the trombones had been guilty of a mésalliance with a bombardon . . . and that the mother of the horns must have run away with a whole military band.' Shaw was undoubtedly aiming to amuse, rather than to be analytical, and the identity of the players is unknown, but some musicians recall a similar shock when, in 1932, Beecham equipped the LPO horn section with German double horns instead of the traditional French-influenced single F horns.

Related instruments

Wagner Tuba

The origins of the Wagner Tuba lie sixty miles to the east of Prague in Königgratz (Hradec Králové), where Červený, the most notable of Bohemia's many indigenous manufacturers, invented a horn substitute known as the Cornon in 1846.[46] This oval or tuba-like instrument may have come to the attention of Wagner, who wrote for something like it in the score of *Das Rheingold* in 1854 and may also have seen similar instruments by Sax in Paris during the previous year. By now, however, he was unable to locate any instruments of this type, and Hans Richter may have suggested that he should commission a new instrument whose bore was wider than a horn's but used a narrow mouthpipe to connect to a horn player's mouthpiece.[47] Wagner visited Alexander's in Mainz to discuss the project in 1862,[48] but is said to have used specially built instruments in 9-foot B♭ and 12-foot F from Moritz of Berlin for the first complete performance of *The Ring* cycle in 1875. Apart from Richard Strauss and Bruckner, few other composers wrote for Wagner tubas, and there was no consensus about notating their parts, but as their bells point to the right and their valves are played by the left hand, they are invariably played by horn players, and anyone who is accustomed to transposition will easily decipher the composer's intentions.

The tenor cor

The tenor cor was invented in about 1860 by Ligner, a member of the band of the French Garde Republicaine, in an attempt to develop an instrument which would look like a horn but whose shorter length would enable it to play in the safer, lower reaches of the harmonic series. It was usually pitched an octave above horn F, but an optional slide allowed it to play in E♭,[49] and it is in this key that tenor cors are most frequently found in this country today. They are, therefore, at the same pitch as the English brass band instrument, the tenor horn, and although the two instruments are configured differently, their mouthpieces are similar. There was never any expectation that the tenor cor player would use his hand in the bell, so the valves are played with the right hand, leaving the left to hold the instrument away from the body. Their shorter length means that their tone is quite unlike that of the horn, but, while junk shops were once full of tenor cors masquerading as French horns, they now seem likely to become historic instruments in their own right.

Accessories

Mouthpieces

The problems associated with mouthpieces are never more difficult to deal with than when they relate to historic instruments. Small in size, they are easily separated from the instrument for which they were intended, are frequently found without a maker's name, and are almost never dated. The slightest change in a mouthpiece can make an immense difference to performance quality, yet they have changed considerably over the years, and few players can afford to play exclusively on historic instruments. Using a modern mouthpiece on an old instrument will deny its full tonal potential, and using a handhorn mouthpiece on a wide-bore double horn will probably have a disastrous effect on intonation, so some compromise between authenticity and practicality is almost inevitable.

6a Typical modern mouthpiece

6b Typical nineteenth-century mouthpiece.

The material from which mouthpieces are made has remained fairly constant: some modern players have experimented with detachable plastic rims, but brass or nickel silver are most common today, and the author of the *New Instructions*[50] confirms that brass was also popular in 1780. He adds, however, that 'some are made of silver, and some of ivory'. This makes no difference to the tone, 'but silver I would give preference to, as brass, when first you apply it to your lips has a disagreeable taste, and ivory often splits, but silver is generally sweet and wholesome'. The diameter of the crosscut (the internal diameter of the mouthpiece at the rim) has also always been a matter of personal taste, and will depend on the thickness of the player's lips and on whether he or she prefers high or low parts.

Other features of mouthpiece construction have, however, changed considerably, with the biggest difference occurring in the depth of the cup and the throat. Modern models almost invariably funnel into a relatively tight throat and then flare out again in the backbore (see Illustration 6a), but surviving piston horn mouthpieces, and drawings in nineteenth-century tutors, show a configuration which is conical and completely lacking in either a tight throat or a flaring back bore (see Illustration 6b). All the French tutors prefer a conical mouthpiece; of the hand horn tutors, only Fröhlich[51] shows a cupped mouthpiece as well, and even that has no flaring back bore.

'Modern' models, with their relatively shallow cup and flaring back bore seem to have been introduced to England by Adolf Borsdorf, for when Tom Busby recalled the horn tone of his youth, he commented,

> There has been considerable alteration of the tone during my career, the old mellow, rich and sweet tone . . . has entirely disappeared, and instead we have a hard, harsh and altogether foreign sound, which to my mind is unrecognisable to one who has heard (and with pleasure too) such players as Van Haute, Stennebruggen, Chas. Harper, William Handley, Tom Mann, William Naldrett, C. Preatoni and Fritz Wendland . . . The change, I am certain, has been brought about by Borsdorf's method of teaching and instruction by him of a mouthpiece with a choked bore which simply kills all possibility of producing the correct sound that one would wish to hear from a horn'.[52]

Naldrett, the first horn in Mann's Crystal Palace Orchestra, clearly made a considerable impact on Busby, for he told Blandford that 'once he entirely forgot to play his part, because he was so rapt in listening to Naldrett'.[53] Blandford conceded that he 'had a lovely tone', but added that he 'never practised'.

The bore of a mouthpiece has a significant effect on the player's sound: the deeper the cup, the richer the resulting tone and, on the lowest crooks, the clearer the sound. Conversely, a tight throat and flaring back bore help to produce brilliance on high notes and, on a wide bore instrument, help to control intonation.

The rim also makes a substantial difference, and Blandford recalls[54] that Charles Clinton, who played at Crystal Palace before the turn of the century, used a mouthpiece with a rim about 'as wide as the edge of a shilling'. This is clearly much narrower than is usual today, but some players argue that this type of design makes it easier to achieve crisper articulation, particularly if there is a relatively sharp angle between the rim and cup of the mouthpiece. The late Neill Sanders, on the other hand, took rim width to an extreme on the basis that this would help with stamina in the loud and strenuous parts written in the twentieth century. The precise measurements of nineteenth-century rims are quoted in a number of tutors, and this information is collated by Morley-Pegge,[55] but in general terms, at between one and a half and three millimetres wide, they were barely half the size of most modern rims.

A compromise which allows players to work with both modern and historic instruments is to use a historically appropriate mouthpiece when playing on period instruments, and to cut down the rim of a modern mouthpiece for use with a modern horn. Keeping the feel of the rim constant means that it is possible to get used to using two cup depths, and while playing with a narrow rim may result in some loss of stamina when playing in a modern brass quintet, it is not as difficult to change to such a mouthpiece as it might seem. On a practical point, Dauprat[56] recommends that 'the rim should be slightly rounded. Flat rims, whether at the interior or exterior present a cutting edge that can injure the lips'.

Mutes

Trumpeters certainly used mutes from the seventeenth century, but we do not know when horn players started to copy them, and the story of Hampel's alleged involvement in the invention of the transposing mute was not written down until 1834.[57] Morley-Pegge is certain that eighteenth-century players could play chromatically even while the mute was in place, and substantiates this by quoting Fröhlich's description of a 'hollow papier mâché ball, about six inches across, with an open neck' which could be inserted in the bell of the horn. Inside this ball was another, 'covered with leather, and with a cord attached to it which hung down from the bell. With this the neck could be more or less fully occluded at will, in the same way as by hand stopping.'

A picture of a mute of this type appears in Adam Wirth's *Praktische, systematisch geordnete Hornschule* of 1877,[58] and although, like all the illustrations in this volume, it is poorly drawn, Fröhlich's 'papier maché ball' with an open neck can be clearly seen. The leather-covered ball seems, however, to have been replaced by a concave plate which seems to have been moved not by a cord but by some kind of rod (see Illustration 7).

Maintenance

Early accounts of instrument maintenance are rare, and usually more notable for their curiosity value than as replacements for modern methods. Lagard's recommendation[59] that players should clean the outside of their instrument with 'finely ground tripoli mixed with alcohol or with oil', has stood the test of time, for modern metal polish is made along

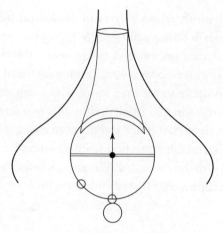

7 Chromatic mute for a hand horn, shown in Adam Wirth's *Praktische, systematische geordnete Hornschule* (1877).

similar lines. However, his suggestion that a solution of caustic potash (potassium hydroxide) is suitable to clean the inside of the horn is positively dangerous: caustic potash is chemically similar to caustic soda, and would cause considerable damage if it came into contact with the player's mouth. Modern valve oil is also preferable to Otto Langey's remedy for sticky valves:[60] 'Unscrew the cap, withdraw the piston and wipe it with an old silk handkerchief kept for that purpose, then expectorate upon the piston and carefully replace it.'

Choice of instrument

Finding the right historic horn is perhaps as big a problem as acquiring the technique needed to play it. Any bargains have long since gone, and the few horns which do come up for sale continually increase in price, so it is most unlikely that anyone will want to play – and carry around – an original instrument from the first half of the nineteenth century or earlier in the hurly-burly of modern life.

Using an original instrument is, in any case, highly impractical in Baroque repertoire. Playing in tune with other musicians is virtually impossible on an instrument with a fixed mouthpipe and no tuning slide, and in most situations a reproduction instrument is the only practical alternative. This may have crooks and tuning bits or, if it was built after about 1981, one or more carefully positioned holes in the main tubing. These 'nodal vents' derive from the reproduction valveless trumpets which have been manufactured since about the 1950s, and were first applied to the horn by the London horn player Timothy Brown. A hole is made in the tube at the point where it would be cut if the horn was to be a fourth higher. Thus, for a horn in F, the hole is nine feet from the mouthpiece, stopping the air column vibrating at the point which is the length of a B♭ alto horn. The player keeps the hole closed until he reaches a naturally out of tune note such as the 11th or 13th harmonic – concert pitch B♭ and D on an F horn – and then lifts his finger, 'converting' the horn to B♭ alto. The same notes can then be played in tune as eighth and tenth harmonics and, unless the player blows very hard, will have a good tone colour because enough air remains inside the horn for the bell to act as a megaphone. John Webb has gone a step further by building a horn with four nodal vents so that it can be played in the most common Baroque keys of G, F, E♭ and D; when using this instrument, the player has to decide before he starts to play which hole to open and which to cover with a screw-threaded cap and washer. The extent to which this principle was applied to the trumpet before the twentieth century is minimal and there is no evidence at all that historic horns were equipped in such a way, so it is entirely spurious in terms of really authentic performance practice. It is, nevertheless, an ingenious solution to an intractable problem.

If, however, you find and are tempted by something looking like an original Baroque horn, check that it is not really a trompe de chasse. Trompes, which are still built today for use by French (and some German) huntsmen, have a fixed mouthpipe, are usually pitched in D, and, as they are held on the player's shoulder, do not have a tuning slide. They are often to be found in the windows of French junk shops, and with their very narrow bore produce the raucous sounds associated with French hunting music.

One way of getting a general – but not infallible – feeling for the date of a horn is to look at the construction of its bell. Most instruments which were made before the beginning of the twentieth century have a triangular piece of brass inserted into the flare, and this two-part construction is usually quite easy to see. However, from the 1930s, American manufacturers led by G.C. Conn[61] adopted the technique of spinning the bell up from a flat disc of brass, and as others quickly followed their example it is most likely that a horn with a seamless bell dates from the twentieth century. This, however, is only a general guide: Alexander are not alone in adding a triangular gusset to some of their instruments today and some earlier builders – such as I.A. Lausmann of Linz[62] – made spun bells in the nineteenth century.

Tuning is not an issue on instruments from the Classical period, but brass is susceptible to corrosion, and original instruments often wear through and become very brittle as the brass reacts with sweaty hands. Soldered joints can also give way, so a reproduction instrument is a sensible choice, but beware some of the early 'copies' which were built twenty to thirty years ago: many bear little resemblance to an original, and some are copies of piston horns which had had their valves removed. They therefore postdate most of the music which will be played on them. More recent copies by makers such as Meinl and Lauber, Paxman, Helmut Finke, Andreas Jungwirth, Engelbert Schmid, Richard Seraphinoff and John Webb are very much better; Webb's instruments have been particularly successful, and include Bohemian and French models of hand horn which he designed in cooperation with Anthony Halstead.

The life of an original nineteenth-century valve horn is likely to be even shorter than that of its predecessors, for when corrosion affects valves they leak and the whole instrument becomes unplayable. The exacting nature of their construction means, however, that reproduction valve horns are virtually unknown, so you may decide to take the risk of repairing a leaky model. Its country of origin may often be inferred from its bore: since the eighteenth century, manufacturers in German and Czech-speaking countries have preferred wider bore instruments, while the French and – until the 1930s – the British, have opted for a narrower one. Once again, however, a note of caution is necessary, for early nineteenth-century instruments by manufacturers such as Courtois and Halary had slightly wider bell throats than some which were made later in the century by Raoux-Millereau in France, and by Hawkes in England. Bear in mind, too, that many of these later horns were built with valves which have since been removed so that they can be passed off as hand horns; the results of doing this can be quite effective, but piston horns are themselves acquiring rarity value and the desecration of so many is deplorable. It is also of limited use, for full sets of crooks are extremely rare; a complete range was still available through Rudall, Carte & Co. Ltd in 1928, but it is unlikely that many were sold.

It is relatively easy to get an early twentieth-century British horn with three Périnet (piston) valves but this may well be a military instrument, and will probably not be exactly right in other respects, for many mid-nineteenth-century French and English players used two-valved horns, Germans preferred a rotary mechanism, and most Austrian horns had Vienna valves. Original horns suitable for playing German Romantic music are rare in this country, but you will sometimes find a French, or French-style, instrument with a sauterelle, a detachable set of valves. Finally, many single F rotary valve instruments which appear to date from the nineteenth century have, in fact, been manufactured since the war for use by beginners.

The art of matching the instrument to the music is clearly extremely difficult. In a 1910 advertisement Tom Busby, first horn at Covent Garden and professor at both Trinity College and the Guildhall School of Music, testifies to the qualities of three-valved horns by Hawkes and Sons,[63] and a fair number of instruments by this company survive today. Franz Paersch, however, preferred a horn by William Brown while he was first horn of the Hallé (1883–1915), and an 1864 catalogue suggests that many London professionals, including Charles Harper, Thomas Mann, James Catchpole, James Standen, Antoine Pacquis, William Handley, Robert Keevil, Waterson, F. Garthwaite, Morgan, and A. Stock used instruments by Raoux-Labbaye.[64] Many of these will have used a combination of two valves and hand horn technique, but in the absence of good original instruments this tradition of performance cannot be revived until reproductions are available.

Collections

Reading about early horns can only ever be second best to looking at and playing them. The museums and collections listed below are worth visiting, but as some are not always open to the public it is best to contact them first to confirm arrangements in advance.

Great Britain

Bate Collection of Musical Instruments, Faculty of Music, University of Oxford, St Aldates, Oxford OX1 1DB

Boosey & Hawkes Museum, Deansbrook Road, Edgware, Middx, HA8 9BB

Edinburgh University Collection of Historic Musical Instruments, Reid Concert Hall, Bristo Square, Teviot Place, Edinburgh, EH8 9AG

Gloucester Folk Museum, 99–103 Westgate Street, Gloucester, GL1 2PG

Horniman Museum and Library, London Road, Forest Hill, London SE23 3PQ

Museum of London, London Wall, London EC2Y 5HN

Rimmer Collection, Wigan Heritage Service, The History Shop, Rodney Street, Wigan, Greater Manchester, WN1 1DQ

Royal College of Music Museum of Instruments, Prince Consort Road, South Kensington, London SW7 2BS

Victoria and Albert Museum: Collection of Musical Instruments, Department of Furniture, Victoria and Albert Museum, Cromwell Road, South Kensington, London SW7 2RL

The Wallace Collection, Manchester Square, London W1M 6BN

Austria

Kunsthistorisches Museum, Sammlung alter Musikinstrumente, Neue Burg A-1010 Wien

Belgium

Brussels Conservatoire, Villa Hermosastraat 1, 1000–Brussels

Germany

Bayerisches Nationalmuseum, Musikinstrumentenmuseum, Münchner Stadtmuseum, St Jakobsplatz, D 80331 München

Musikinstrumenten-Museum der Karl-Marx-Universität, Täubschenweg 2c, D 04193, Leipzig

Musikinstrumenten-Museum, Bienengarten 2, D 08258, Markneukirchen

Musikinstrumenten-Museum, Staatliches Instituts für Musikforschung, Preussischer Kulturbesitz, Tiergartenstrasse 1, D 10785 Berlin-Tiergarten

France

Paris Conservatoire Museum, 209 Avenue Jean Jaurès, 75109-Paris

USA

America's Shrine to Music Museum, The University of South Dakota, 414 East Clark Street, Vermillion, SD 57069-2390

Smithsonian Institute, SI Building, Washington DC 20560-0010

4 Technique

Tutors

The few eighteenth-century horn tutors offer little help in terms of the specifics of technique, for most were published in the relative isolation of England, and derive from *The Compleat Tutor*, the earliest known work of its type for the horn, and one which does little more than cover the basics. It was first published in London by John Simpson in 1746[1] and was probably written by Christopher[2] Winch, a player who performed in 'Mr Handel's operas and oratorios for several years'.[3] It was published again as *The French Horn Master*[4] in about 1750, reappeared in an almost exact reprint in 1756 in an edition by Peter Thompson, and then surfaced again under the title, *Instructions for the French Horn*, in 1757 as part of a series of tutors known collectively as *Apollo's Cabinet*.[5] In this form it seems to have had a reasonable circulation – in about 1780, an anonymous 'eminent performer' quoted it verbatim in parts of the *New Instructions for the French Horn*[6] – but by now the original text was over thirty years old, and so may not represent the most up-to-date ideas on performance practice. It is tempting to think that the author's greatest expertise may have related to the horn as an outdoor instrument for he begins with a rêverie on the beauties of the horn 'on the water or near the side of cliffs or hanging woods' and as an aid to 'diverting the hunters'. He also includes a number of hunting calls and suggests that the instrument's 'bawling' tone is inappropriate to concerts.

While it is possible that Baroque horn technique could have been learned – by trumpeters in particular – without the help of detailed tutors, it is surprising that hand stopping should have remained almost undocumented until the very end of the eighteenth century. Hampel's failure to describe it in writing may indicate that he thought it unnecessary to do so, or that he did not really invent the technique, or that he did and was guarding his secret jealously. A detailed description of hand stopping eventually occurs in 1797 in the tutor by Spandau's Flemish pupil, Othon Vandenbroek,[7] and, during the next few years, the technique was covered in enormous detail by the Parisian players. Frédéric Duvernoy's *Méthode pour le Cor* of 1803[8] might today seem quite comprehensive had it not been followed in 1807 by Heinrich Domnich's *Méthode de Premier et de Second Cor* and then, in 1824, by Louis-François Dauprat's blockbuster, the *Méthode de Cor Alto et de Cor Basse*. Pierre-Joseph Meifred wrote a tutor for a two-valved horn in 1841, publishing a new edition for instruments with three valves in 1849, and others who wrote for valve horns include Kastner (1840),[9] Gounod (1845),[10] Haumuller (1845)[11] and Urbin (1852).[12] The French players' loyalty to the hand horn meant that it was still worthwhile to produce tutors for the valveless instrument for most of the century, and those who did so include Jacqmin (1832),[13] Mengal (1835),[14] Gallay (1845),[15] Blanc (1855),[16] Mohr (1871)[17] and finally Lagard (1878).[18]

The French tutors are unrivalled by any publication from other countries, but while Franz Joseph Fröhlich did not play the horn himself, it is clear from the short and very interesting instruction book which he published in Bonn in 1811[19] that he was advised by someone who understood the instrument very well indeed. Other early tutors from German-speaking Europe include J.H. Göroldt's *Hornschule* of 1822[20] and the *Hornschule* by the Viennese bandmaster, Andreas Nemetz, which appeared in 1829.[21]

Holding the instrument

The author of the *New Instructions*,[22] advises that the horn is usually held 'with the right hand nearly in the middle of the Hoop, the Bell hanging over the same arm'. This stance would have allowed hunting horn players on horseback to hold the reins in one hand and the instrument in the other. The author adds, however, that 'it would be absurd to adopt only one peculiar method, as different positions will hereafter be found very convenient and absolutely necessary', and in a section which hints at an understanding of hand stopping, points out that 'should you want to make the cromatic tones, [sic] . . . one hand must be within the edge of the Bell ready to put into the Pavilion or Bell of the horn as the notes require'. This suggests the modern way of holding the instrument, but the horn is also 'sometimes' held with the bell 'perpendicular, which . . . method is generally used in concerts'. This is corroborated by many eighteenth-century pictures of players

8 Frontispiece from *The Compleat Tutor* (London: John Simpson, 1746).
Although the instrument is not particularly well drawn, it shows the posi-
tion for holding the horn which is recommended in the text. (London,
British Library, d.47 f(5))

holding a horn in one hand and the bell in the air, and Dauprat claims that 'in the theatres in some towns near Milan, and even in the region's capital itself', he had seen 'players holding the bells of their horns up in the air' during loud passages.[23] However, this position is far from practical: with its bell in the air, even a lightweight Baroque horn quickly becomes unbearably heavy, any terminal crooks begin to become loose, and bubbles of condensation run back into the player's mouth.

In the Baroque, when appearance was important, horns were often built to be played in pairs, with one player holding his instrument in his right hand and the other in the left. 'Reverse', or 'left-handed' designs continued to be made until the early twentieth century, and a celebrated example is the Raoux cor solo which is now in the Victoria and Albert Museum and was once the property of Giovanni Puzzi. Dauprat recorded that 'most German virtuosi whom we have seen in Paris hold it this way',[24] but while Fröhlich says that the horn is held 'more commonly with the left hand', he adds that 'whoever is studying to be a first horn should accustom himself to holding the horn with his right hand so that when playing duets the bells of the two horns are side-by-side and each can hear the other better'.[25] Tully, too, regards the left-handed design as normal, advising that players 'fix the right hand close to the stay of the crook . . . [and] at the same time place the left hand a little way in at the bottom part of the bell'.[26] François Brémond,[27] the English player Hinchcliffe, and Emile Lamouret and Edmond Entraigue, the first and third horns at the Paris Opéra, still preferred to hold the horn with their right hands towards the end of the nineteenth century, but most players preferred to learn the skill of hand stopping with the right hand, and to give the left hand the easier job of holding the instrument. The survival of hand stopping well into the valve horn era ensured that the horn became the only modern brass instrument whose valves are usually played with the left hand.

Control of intonation

It is a feature of the harmonic series that several notes – most particularly the 7th, 11th and 13th harmonics, written as B♭, F and A – sound horribly out of tune. Such notes were part and parcel of the hunt, and are still played untempered on the trompe de chasse today, but while it is unlikely that such intonation was welcomed when the horn joined other instruments in the concert hall, we do not know how players adjusted it. One of the most significant issues for horn players today – and one of the hardest to answer – is how players controlled intonation in the pre-hand-horn era.

It is possible that horn players followed the precedent of their trumpet playing colleagues, and tried to 'lip' out-of-tune notes into place, for bending notes to a different pitch by slightly changing the embouchure had been necessary on the trumpet since Girolamo Fantini included a large number of non-harmonic notes in his sonatas during the first half of the seventeenth century.[28] Modern trumpeters' tone quality usually suffers when they try to bend notes, and it is even more difficult to do so on a horn, but as Baroque players often performed on both instruments, and their parts are frequently indistinguishable, horn players almost certainly knew of the technique and tried it out.

Players whose bells pointed over their shoulders would not have thought of holding the inside of the bell, but those whose instrument was configured on more modern lines had a good chance of discovering that they could affect tuning by obscuring part of the bell. The relatively small bell throat on Baroque horns meant that the instrument made particularly unpleasant sounds if the player inserted his hand, but the fingers may have been used to improve the intonation of the most unruly notes.

Tessitura

Composers who wanted the horn to play melodic passages were forced by the gaps in the harmonic series to write at the top of its range. Players who were also trumpeters would have taken such parts in their stride, but today many players are initially horrified – even when they are equipped with modern instruments – at the extreme tessitura which is characteristic of the Baroque and early Classical periods. Without any mid-range lyrical works to play, however, eighteenth-century players could turn their entire attention to mastering the highest range of the instrument, and Barry Tuckwell took the same approach when he was faced with recording Zelenka's extremely high Capriccios, concentrating exclusively on the top end of his register for a fortnight.[29] Few players have the luxury of being able to neglect the rest of their technique for so long, however, and the range of some solo parts therefore remains immensely challenging.

Hand stopping

How hand stopping works

Many explanations of hand stopping are written by authors who are expert as horn players or as acousticians, but not as both. In contrast, Richard Merewether was both a fine horn player and chief designer for Paxman Musical Instruments, and his book, *The Horn, the Horn*, includes one of the best and clearest descriptions of this complex subject.[30]

A first important principle is that although hand stopping does not work in cylindrical tubes, the acoustical properties of conical tubes make it possible to lower the pitch of any open harmonic by completely 'stopping' the tube with the hand. The extent to which the pitch is lowered depends on the length of tube in the instrument, but on a horn built in the 'soloists' keys' of F, E, E♭ or D the result of completely stopping any harmonic will be to produce a note which is almost exactly a semitone above the next harmonic down. In instruments pitched in lower keys, the resulting note is less than a semitone above the next harmonic down, while on higher crooks it is greater.

The player who forms a note on one of the 'soloists' crooks', and then simultaneously hand stops and blows a little harder, feels a slight click in the embouchure as the note rises by a semitone. This suggests that hand stopping shortens the tube and therefore raises the pitch of the harmonics, but the following experiment proves otherwise:

(1) On an F horn, play the fifth harmonic (bottom line E)
(2) Hand stop fully and and at the same time blow slightly harder; the pitch moves up a semitone to F.
(3) Continue to play F, but gradually move the right hand back to the open position: the note moves up through F♯ to G, the 6th harmonic. Thus the F was actually a lowered 6th harmonic, sounding a semitone above the 5th.

The experiment can also be done in reverse:

(1) On an F horn, play the sixth harmonic (G)
(2) Gradually stop the note – but don't blow harder – and it will fall first to
     F♯ and then to F.

Right hand technique

To play the hand horn well, the player's hand needs to be big enough
to stop the bell completely; players who find this difficult on a modern
instrument should remember that the bell throat is usually narrower on
hand horns. The correct hand position, however, is much the same on both
instruments : 'Four fingers are brought together and pressed lightly against
each other', wrote Dauprat.[31]

> The top of the hand is rounded, the palm is cupped, the *thenar*
> [the ball of muscle at the base of the thumb] and *hypothenar* [the
> palm of the hand] are brought towards each other, and the thumb,
> making a backward motion, is bent at its first joint to rest at the
> base of the index finger. After forming the hand thus, it is inserted
> into the bell so that the middle sections of the index, middle and
> ring fingers touch the interior of the bell on its right side, whether
> in the open or stopped postion. That is to say, once the hand is in
> this position, it makes no further movement other than that neces-
> sary to close the bell to varying degrees by pressing with the *thenar*
> and lowest part of the *hypothenar* to the left. This movement
> pushes back the tips of the fingers against the right interior of the
> bell but does not disturb the middle joints. These do not change
> their place even for the very open notes, for the execution of which
> the hand spreads out and stretches a little in order to enlarge the
> opening. Finally, the hand, in relation to the arm, remains in its
> natural position.

The only question outstanding is how far inside the bell the hand should
be placed. Gallay suggests that the thumb should be close to the stay which
joins the bell to the hoop of the horn;[32] experiments with a French instrument of the period suggest that this position is slightly further into the bell

than is usual on the modern horn, but minimises the hand movement which is needed to move between open and stopped notes. Interestingly, however, Gallay also suggests keeping a space of about four centimetres between the hand and the left hand side of the bell. This very open position results in comparatively harsh stopped sounds, but ensures that they can be heard as such by the audience. A smaller gap results in a slightly more veiled tone on the open notes and helps to equalise the sound of the stopped notes, but can make them inaudible to the audience. The pragmatic solution which is usually adopted today is explained by Duvernoy:[33] 'Notes which are played without placing the hand in the bell are naturally louder and more sonorous than those where it is necessary to stop the bell; to avoid this drawback it is therefore necessary to hold back the loud notes to hear the weak ones, and endeavour to give equality to all sounds alike.' Fröhlich[34] notes that 'special care should be taken not to force the stopped notes too much for this can produce unpleasant sounds', and recommends that, 'In order to obtain equality one should leave the hand in the horn when playing the good notes.' Despite such optimism, however, it has always been recognised that it was neither possible, nor even entirely desirable, to smooth out open and stopped sounds completely.

Learning to hand stop

There is plenty of evidence that both professional players and other writers thought that hand horn technique took a long time to learn. Heinrich Domnich[35] asserts that mastering its complete range takes 'several years of unrelenting study', and most of the French nineteenth-century tutors assume that the novice pupil will find it very much easier to learn a wide range of open notes than to learn to hand stop. In fact, it is easier to learn to hand stop around the 'easier' open notes than it is to play high or low open notes well, but Duvernoy's course starts with a C major arpeggio and in lesson 7 moves on to fourth line D. The pupil learns to use the hand to flatten this, but when he reaches top line F in lesson 11 he will be far more worried by its tessitura than by the hand movement needed to play it. He eventually progresses to the comparatively easy middle register stopped notes only after learning the factitious notes.

Dauprat shows more understanding, pointing out that hands and instruments vary in size, and that 'certain stopped notes (such as, for example, the

D below the first line of the staff, and the F just above) sometimes resist the efforts of beginners for quite a long time, and this may make them feel disgusted with an instrument whose imperfections they learn before they experience its beauties and advantages'.[36] He also understands the need to teach beginners to compromise between the ringing quality of open notes and the muffled sound of stopped ones so that they avoid 'offensive inequality'. The early lessons still cover the entire range of the instrument from pedal notes to the D above the staff, but Dauprat points out that learning to hand stop involves trial and error, 'listening acutely', getting a feel for the instrument in general and discovering the characteristics of each crook in particular.

As the player cannot see his hand in the bell, his success as a hand horn player will depend mainly on experience and the extent to which he feels at home with the instrument. Diagrams showing the extent to which notes need to be stopped often help, however, and the chart shown overleaf as Example 4.1 is intended as a starting point for players who are beginning to experiment with the hand horn. I have not attempted to distinguish between enharmonic equivalents (F♯ and G♭, for example), as the nineteenth-century tutors do not agree with each other about the hand positions which are involved, and modern ears are firmly gripped by equal temperament. The chart frequently reflects the advice of the nineteenth-century writers, but the technique of hand stopping is not an exact science, and while I have called upon my own experience in developing it, other experienced players will have refinements of their own. As Dauprat wrote, all hand positions 'must be submitted to the judgment of the ear. A hand that is too large or too small, a bell that is more or less spacious, the crook on which one plays and the key in which the music is composed, may all compel one to modify these signs one way or the other.'[37]

The first six notes (*Octave 1*) are not members of the harmonic series, but it is easy to lip them down from the open C and they are rarely approached in any other way. The eighth note, the C♯ immediately above low C (*Octave 2*), is unusual, but in slow passages can easily be produced by lipping C upwards and removing the hand from the bell. It can also be produced as a rather muffled stopped note. Some tutors show the next semitone up, low D, as a stopped note, but generally speaking it is so weak as to be impractical, and Dauprat omits it from his chart. D♯, E, F and F♯ can all be produced, increasingly clearly, by stopping low G. More experienced players may also be able

Example 4.1 Chart showing approximate hand positions. Appropriate for a player with an average hand size, and using a horn equipped with an E♭ crook.

Key:
O = Open
F = Fully stopped
W = Wide open
W/F = Either wide open or fully stopped
I = Impractical
1/2 = Half stopped
3/4 = Three-quarters stopped

N.B. Notes given in bass clef use old notation i.e. they sound a fourth above their written pitch. Although this convention seems illogical, and had critics as early as 1830 when London's Harmonicon magazine published a letter from "H.C." on the subject, it is still widely used today.

to produce them as open notes – especially in slow passages – by lipping down the G, but this is more difficult than lipping down from low C. E, F and F♯ are worth practising as they appear fairly frequently in hand-horn repertoire; Fröhlich advises that 'E is not impossible on many horns, but it never makes the horn vibrate in such a way that it can make a proper sound. One can also play the F without stopping . . . if it responds it is necessarily stronger and brighter than when it is stopped, but players should only adopt this expedient when playing in slow time.'[38]

A reasonable G♯ can be played by bending the G upwards and removing the hand from the bell, and although neither A nor B♭ is ever very successful,

Example 4.2 Franz Danzi: Sonata in E minor, Op. 44. Opening of first movement.

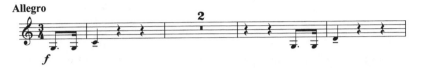

Horn in E

they appear only rarely and can usually be played by using fairly heavy hand-stopping. The A does appear in Reicha's Trios, op. 82, however, and is easiest to play when it is approached from the C above. Moving into the third octave, C♯ and D are not easy to play, but work quite well in the context of a descending chromatic scale. Cultivating a convincing D is essential for it occurs frequently in parts written after about 1800, and while it presents few problems in well-prepared quick passages, there are occasions, such as the opening of Danzi's E minor Sonata, op. 44, where it is horribly exposed (see Example 4.2).

From E upwards is the hand horn's best range, though it can be tricky to sound F effectively. A slightly different hand position is needed to get 2nd space A and 3rd line B in tune, and B♭, the seventh harmonic, must be played with a very open hand position to avoid sounding flat. In the fourth octave, C, D and E are all open notes, but the hand has to be used very slightly both to flatten the naturally sharp D, and to sharpen the naturally flat E.

Top line F♯ and the A above the stave are notoriously difficult, and to Domnich they were 'the most difficult to play in tune, especially when found in isolated instances'.[39] No tutor suggests anything other than an approximate way of playing them, so I have included two possible hand positions. It is important to remember that in some contexts it is permissible to mislead the audience: writing of the passage shown in Example 4.3, Dauprat observed that, 'only the first and fourth notes of each beat are considered in determining the motion of the hand'[40] and at sufficient speed it is indeed possible to fool the ear into thinking that it heard the intervening notes even though the necessary hand movement is impossible in the time available.

Example 4.3 Dauprat: *Méthode*, p. 206.

Hand horn players soon develop a feeling for what is, and what is not, good writing for the instrument, but even experienced performers are sometimes astonished at nineteenth-century writers' blasé approach to major difficulties. Some of the studies in their tutors are so difficult that they would be very challenging to play even on the modern horn, but the number of very difficult studies in the tutors suggests that their writers had high expectations of their pupils, and there must have been a considerable number of players whose technique was truly astonishing.

Hand stopping on the valve horn

Many writers identified the possibility of using hand stopping as a way of combining the tonal variety of the hand horn with the chromatic flexibility of the valve horn, and Meifred saw valves as a device which would give the player more control over the use of stopped notes. He recommends, for example, that on the valve horn, leading notes should be lightly stopped, and resolve onto an open tonic[41] (see Example 4.4) and also points out that different valve combinations allow players to control the degree of stopping required on any particular note. Franz Ludwig Schubert[42] places considerable importance on the need to reflect the composer's intentions, and says that, 'when it is clear that [he] has chosen a stopped note for a particular effect', it would be wrong to use the valves to make an open sound. Even Oskar Franz, the author of one of the 'first modern methods', was, according to Borsdorf, 'very chary about allowing his pupils to use the valves on the valve horn when a good note could be obtained without them. Such a phrase as [Example 4.5] had to be played with the hand alone.'[43] The conventions for marking notes which should be stopped are explained by Wagner: 'The individual notes marked with a + indicate stopped tones; even if these occur on notes which are open, it is still assumed that the player will, on each occasion, change the pitch by means of a valve in such a way that the intended tone sounds like a stopped note.'[44]

Example 4.4 Meifred: *Méthode pour le cor chromatique ou à pistons*, p. 32.

Example 4.5.

Embouchure

The components of embouchure – note production, mouthpiece placement, and pressure – receive varied amounts of attention in the tutors. There is some agreement on the question of note production: Jean Mengal voices the general rule when he tells players not to 'puff out the cheeks',[45] and *The Compleat Tutor* recommends that they 'Observe as the Notes rise to pinch the Lips and likewise express each Note with the Tip of the Tongue'.[46] *The Compleat Tutor* also advises the player to 'draw in your cheeks, that you may have a greater Command of the Instrument'. No such consensus exists, however, on the question of mouthpiece position, and some tutors recommend a different placement depending on whether the player is a cor basse or cor alto. Domnich, for example, suggests that low players 'place two thirds of the mouthpiece on the upper lip and the other third on the lower', and that while high players will usually position it centrally, 'a few apply only a third of the mouthpiece to their top lip with the other two thirds on the lower lip'.[47]

Others consider that the player's preferred tessitura makes no difference. Both *The Compleat Tutor*, and *New Instructions* recommend, rather simplistically, that the mouthpiece should be placed 'about the centre of your lips', with 'not too much of the upper nor too much of the under lip',[48] but Tully prefers it to be 'against the centre of the mouth nearly, but rather more on the lower than the upper lip'.[49] A different type of placement, known as 'einsetzen', is described by Oskar Franz,[50] and involves resting the edge of the mouthpiece in the red flesh of the lower lip. Fitzpatrick[51] offers, but does not substantiate, the theory that this technique goes back to Hampel, and while it certainly seems to have been adopted by low horn specialists, Barry Tuckwell[52] points out that it was also favoured by both Dennis and Aubrey Brain.

For the most part, the nineteenth-century tutors recommend that the mouthpiece should be positioned with two-thirds of it against the upper lip and a third on the lower. This, of course, remains the norm today, and to Dauprat the rationale is that here

> it naturally finds a point of support which will prevent it from changing position . . . Since the mouthpiece must always have support against the lips, most cor basse players bring their lower jaw forward slightly. The lips are thus tightened on both sides of the mouthpiece while leaving sufficient opening in the centre of the mouth to permit this large volume of air to pass completely into the instrument with no loss at the sides.[53]

New Instructions alone makes the pragmatic comment that that an off-centre [i.e. left/right] embouchure may be necessary in players whose teeth 'do not stand quite equal'.[54]

Dauprat's views are often well thought out, but on the matter of mouthpiece pressure he is controversial, suggesting that pitch 'depends upon the amount of pressure the mouthpiece exerts on the lips. The stronger this pressure is, the more the lips are tightened and the air passage is narrowed.' Domnich shares this opinion, and Baines[55] suggests that the modern technique of buzzing notes without pressure developed among brass band players only at the beginning of the twentieth century. In a different part of his tutor, however, Dauprat seems to contradict himself, commenting that 'the poise of the mouthpiece is the most gracious to the sight, leaving the expression and all the muscles of the face in a perfect state of rest'.[56] This does not sound like a recipe for a tight, smiling embouchure, and Sax[57] and

Fröhlich[58] certainly dissented from the 'press and hope' approach: 'The easier and freer the embouchure', wrote Fröhlich,'the less breath the player needs to cultivate a full tone, the less he needs to press the mouthpiece against his lips, the greater their freedom of play, the closer he has come towards perfecting a good embouchure. The player also benefits because the hard pressure of the mouthpiece does not tire his lips too soon.' This is clearly common sense, and even if we were to discover that a pressured embouchure was typical of the nineteenth century, modern players might decide that pragmatism, and the need for stamina, dictate against its use today.

Breathing

Although correct breathing is clearly fundamental to good brass playing, many of the nineteenth-century tutors omit it completely, and none gives it much attention. Lagard[59] recommends that 'the intake of air needs to be effected from the base of the chest. Inspiration from the upper chest does not reach the same target and produces ungraceful movements of the shoulders.' Dauprat quotes a passage from the singing tutor which Bernardo Mengozzi wrote for the Paris Conservatoire: 'When inhaling it is necessary to flatten the abdomen and raise it quickly, expanding and extending the chest. While exhaling the abdomen must return very slowly to its natural condition and the chest must fall at the same rate, so as to conserve and manage the air in the lungs as long as possible.'[60] Quantz[61] offers similar advice for flautists:

> To play long passage-work you must slowly inhale a good supply of breath. To this end you must enlarge your throat and expand your chest fully, draw up your shoulders, and try to retain the breath in your chest as fully as possible, blowing it very economically. But if you still find it necessary to take breath between quick notes you must make the preceding note very short, inhale the breath rapidly only as far as the throat, and rush the following two or three notes a little so that the beat is not retarded, and none of the notes is omitted.

It is clearly not acceptable to dismiss any statement just because it disagrees with modern practice, but in the absence of any other advice it is probably sensible to ignore such puzzling statements and to apply the best of today's methods to issues relating to breathing.

Tonguing

There is disagreement about the syllable which the player should imagine while tonguing, and while this problem quickly becomes a historical nicety, the tutors' various solutions may tell us something about their mental image of tone quality. Punto[62] recommends 'daon' on a strongly tongued note, 'ta' for staccato and 'da' for softly tongued notes in Adagios. Dauprat agrees with this in theory, but then points out that in practice the issue is irrelevant as tonguing and speaking are mutually exclusive.[63] Domnich suggests 'tou' or 'dou'[64] but Gallay[65] disagrees, saying Duvernoy's 'tu' is the only acceptable syllable. Dauprat also makes the surprising comment that 'horns only use single tonguing and not the double tonguing employed by trumpets.'[66]

Lip trills

Trills are intrinsic to much eighteenth- and early nineteenth-century music, and without valves, players had no choice but to master the skill of lip trilling. All of the important French tutors include a section on the subject, but none offers a magic formula for success; instead, the general opinion is that the technique takes time and practice, and that the best solution is to start slowly and to build up speed. Dauprat, however, is in two minds: 'Do not hurry to speed up a trill', he writes, but then adds that slow practice is of no use as it 'removes the trilling effect'.[67]

Trills between two open notes are naturally the easiest to master, but as composers wrote others as well, players also needed to develop a suitable hand technique. 'If the main note is natural and the auxiliary note . . . is stopped', writes Dauprat, 'the first is played normally, then the hand closes the bell on the second, opens again, closes again and so on up to speed, after which it is not involved until the termination.' If, however, the main note is stopped and the auxiliary note open, the hand movement will be the reverse: that is, the hand is placed appropriately for the first note, opening and closing the bell alternately at first, and then staying in place once the two notes of the trill are sufficiently adjusted to each other and have become so fast that the hand cannot keep pace with them . . . One can deceive the listener even more certainly if both notes are heard distinctly in both the preparation and the termination of the trill.

Predictably, Dauprat recommends that the hand remains constant if the trill involves two stopped notes, and says that even two differently stopped notes are easier to play than trills which involve one open note.[68]

Mengal,[69] Domnich,[70] Fröhlich,[71] and Klotz[72] quote the conventional line that the tongue rests still during a trill, but Gallay has a more interesting approach: 'On the contrary, it is the tongue, and the tongue alone which works to produce the trill.' [73] He does not, however, suggest that the tip of the tongue should move, and what Fitzpatrick describes as 'a curious manner of fluttering the tongue',[74] may be explained by Philip Farkas[75] and John Ridgeon,[76] who point out that brass players often change the shape of their mouths from the syllable 'aw' on low notes to 'ee' for high ones. Such a large movement is not necessary in a trill, where 'ah-ee-ah-ee-ah-ee' is a better solution; this requires the tongue to oscillate flexibly in the middle, and removes the need for cumbersome and undesirable movements at the corners of the embouchure.

5   The language of musical style

Communication has to involve at least two people, one to create and one to receive. Where the participants have the opportunity to interact there is a reasonable chance that they can make their full meaning understood, but any form of written message is far less precise. Even poets, novelists and artists, who generally communicate with their audiences direct, cannot be entirely sure that their work will be completely understood; composers and playwrights have to rely on the pivotal rôle of intermediaries to give audiences a sympathetic interpretation of their work. Great performances always have an indefinable spark which communicates with the listener and touches his soul, but today they also often reveal an understanding of historical conventions, and the purpose of this chapter is to focus on the kind of interpretative and stylistic issues which horn players need to recognise as part of the process of bringing a silent page of manuscript to life.

Dauprat pays considerable attention to the rôle of the performer, writing that a musical score is

> a text which he explains and comments upon in order to make its
> ideas more apparent and easier to understand. The composer can
> only indicate his intentions, or give a hint of them through the
> conventional signs of tempi and dynamics. It is for the musician to
> enter into the spirit of the music, to identify himself, so to speak,
> with the composer and his works, so that he can render them faithfully in his performance, which is itself, a kind of creation.[1]

The performer therefore has a great responsibility to the composer and listener as well as to himself, and while the composer can help – Elgar, for example, qualified almost every note of his scores with slurs, dots, accents or dynamics – these markings are as inexact as any other form of writing, and have done little to prevent performances of Elgar's music from changing considerably over the last seventy years.

68

Regional variations in sound

World-wide developments in instrument manufacture and recording technology mean that today regional variations of sound are gradually disappearing, but recordings made before the 1960s often reveal horn playing which sounds very different from today's norm. Instrument design accounts for many national stylistic characteristics: German horn players' traditionally heavy tone colour derives from their instruments' fairly large bell throats, narrower bores produce the bright sound which is preserved on many recordings of French players, and English players have arrived at a compromise with a tone which is lighter than the German and less strident than the French.

Descriptions of players' sounds are extremely rare in the nineteenth century, and it is not always clear whether they reflect prejudices against individuals' playing or against national traits. Duvernoy thought his sound 'perfect', but to the Finnish composer and clarinettist Bernhard Crusell, it was 'peculiar'[2] and the Dane Rudolph Bay[3] found it 'shrill and trumpet-like'. His compatriot N.C.L. Abrahams found Gallay's tone 'charming'[4] but Bay[5] greatly preferred the sound made by Johan Andersen, who played in the Copenhagen Opera Orchestra, and the German, Johann Christoph Schuncke, who visited Scandinavia in 1814.

Books

In addition to the specifically horn-related books listed in chapter 1, there are a number of titles which give a general overview of style and interpretation throughout the ages and across national boundaries. Arnold Dolmetsch's *The Interpretation of Music of the seventeenth and eighteenth Centuries*[6] remains a classic, and more recent publications such as Robert Donington's *The Interpretation of Early Music*[7] and Thurston Dart's *The Interpretation of Music*[8] also contain stimulating ideas. Much of their content inevitably falls outside the horn player's repertoire, but they are a valuable source of background information. Other books which deal with more specific issues include *Performance Practice: Music after 1600* – one of the New Grove Handbooks in Music[9] – *The Classical Style* by Charles Rosen,[10] and two titles by F. Neumann, *Ornamentation in Baroque and Post-Baroque Music, with Special Emphasis on J.S. Bach*[11] and *Ornamentation and*

Improvisation in Mozart.[12] A more recent addition to the literature is *The Historical Performance of Music: An Introduction*, by Colin Lawson and Robin Stowell.[13]

Contemporary tutors

The technique-related content of eighteenth- and nineteenth-century tutors for the horn is covered in Chapter 4, but the eighteenth-century tutors which J.J. Quantz,[14] C.P.E. Bach[15] and Leopold Mozart[16] wrote for their own instruments – flute, keyboard and violin – include a considerable amount of general musical and stylistic information and are ideal for mid-eighteenth-century repertoire. They predate the music of Mozart and Haydn, but while Daniel Gottlob Türk's *School of Clavier Playing* of 1789[17] includes additional information on ornamentation and general interpretation, some of their content is the same. Dauprat's horn tutor[18] of 1824 overflows with information on contemporary performance practice, but it is slightly too late to be infallible on the interpretation of the late eighteenth-century composers, and, as it does not include any references to Mozart's works for horn and orchestra, it is possible that Dauprat did not know of their existence.

Domnich,[19] Gallay[20] and Meifred[21] cover general stylistic issues only in very broad terms, and later horn tutors limit themselves almost entirely to technical matters. This may be partly explained by wider philosophical thinking, for while eighteenth-century artists were concerned with reason, rational thought and the need to overcome superstition and prejudice by raising the general level of education, nineteenth-century Romanticism sought to free the human spirit, to re-assert individuality of expression and to give full rein to the imagination. In this culture didactic writing seemed out of place.

This is not to say that personal interpretations were discouraged in the eighteenth century. C.P.E. Bach, for example, advised musicians to play 'from the soul, not like a trained bird. A musician cannot move others unless he too is moved.'[22] Ornamentation is described repeatedly by the eighteenth-century writers as a way of adding 'passion' to an interpretation, but more 'contrived' expression was anathema to Dauprat, who warns players against trying 'to give the impression of being inspired'[23] with 'acquiescing gestures of the arms, rounding in of the shoulders, and rolling of the eyes'. He also advises against tapping the feet while playing,[24] a practice which Türk had commended thirty-five years earlier.[25] Sucking water out of the instrument is 'disagreeable to the audience, because of both the resulting noise and its air of vulgarity',[26] and 'preluding' – or doodling before the start of a piece – is so unacceptable that Dauprat even bans tuning up in public: 'one should hide the means and show only the results'. He does accept that 'solitary preluding', or warming up in private, 'establishes the tuning of the instrument, and gives the lip suppleness and the fingers dexterity', but it should be completed off-stage: 'If you go on and on before the public, whether to amuse yourself, pass the time or show off, you can only bore the listeners and make a fool of yourself.'[27] As the nineteenth century moved on, however, such idiosyncrasies became part of the mystique surrounding the performer.

Some stylistic issues

Vibrato

The evidence for or against vibrato on the horn in the mid-eighteenth century is negligible, and although it may be possible to learn from the changing practice of other musicians, Dauprat warns that such comparisons can be dangerous, citing the 'vogue'[28] among Italian singers for 'starting a note flat and sliding up to pitch, or glissandoing between pairs of notes, or moving from one note to another via the note above the second one'. They 'use this – or rather, they over-use it – in all kinds of music, but especially in recitative. We mention it here only in order to discourage musicians who might seek to use it on their instruments.'

The need for care in drawing parallels between instruments is demonstrable today in the varying conventions concerning vibrato, for while players in British brass bands and in orchestral string sections use it all the time, it is almost unheard of among orchestral horns in the United Kingdom. Leopold Mozart's view of vibrato, however, is temperance itself:[29] 'It would be a mistake to play every note with vibrato', he writes, adding that those who do so sound as though they have 'the palsy'. He adds that 'good instrumentalists' and 'clever singers' apply it 'charmingly' on long notes, and

Quantz, the flautist, felt similarly:[30] 'If you have to hold a long note for either a whole or a half bar, tongue it gently, scarcely exhaling; then allow the strength of the tone to swell from pianissimo to the middle of the note, and back again to the end, making a vibrato with the finger on the nearest open hole.' Horn players who choose to adopt these principles can imitate Quantz's advice on long flute notes by replacing the finger technique with a relaxed, breathy, vibrato, and it is equally possible to follow Leopold Mozart's recommendation that, on the long note before a cadenza, 'an increasing oscillation'[31] should crescendo and then decrescendo.

Fitzpatrick suggests that by 1796 some horn players had mastered vibrato very convincingly, quoting a source which says that it 'can be produced on no other instrument with such expressiveness and vigour as on the horn. The virtuoso has much to overcome in the way of embouchure and pitching, but he also has at his command a wonderful array of melting, floating and dying-away effects'.[32] This is an isolated reference, however, and there is nothing comparable to help players of nineteenth-century music. Spohr follows his eighteenth-century predecessors by advising in his Violin-Schule[33] that 'the deviation from the perfect intonation of the note should hardly be perceptible to the ear', and recommends that it is appropriate on 'strongly accented notes' as well as 'sustained notes in passages of deep passion'. Giovanni Puzzi frequently claimed to perform 'in the style of' the great Italian tenor, Giovanni Battista Rubini, a singer who was renowned for his pronounced vibrato,[34] but recordings show that Edouard Vuillermoz, Professor of horn at the Paris Conservatoire, cultivated a gentle, almost completely straight, sound. This may have been compatible with German orchestral sounds, for, on 23 May 1906, he was joined by Jean Pénable, Jacques Capdevielle and Arthur Delgrange in a performance of Schumann's Conzertstück with the Berlin Philharmonic Orchestra.[35] In contrast, contemporary recordings of trompes de chasse reveal a big vibrato, and as there was a revival of interest in trompes in the 1920s it is possible that they influenced the characteristic wide, insistent vibrato and saxophone-like sound which was adopted by mid-twentieth-century French players such as Jean Devémy, Lucien Thévet and Georges Barboteu. Which, if either, of the two styles was more typical of French playing in the nineteenth century is unknown, but it would probably be as wrong to rule vibrato out of period performances as it would be to use it all the time, and it is not difficult to find places where it is attractive as an expressive device.

Tone quality

Despite Dauprat's hesitations, horn players were frequently advised to copy singers: Morley-Pegge[36] recalls that Emile Lambert, the solo horn with the Lamoreux Orchestra in Paris, had 'a manner of singing on the horn like the uncultured Italian tenor – not knowing how he did it, nor why – and it was a pure joy to listen to him coming through the orchestra as clear as a bell'. Fröhlich,[37] too, remarked that 'If one listens to many good singers, studies songs and constantly strives to train oneself according to true vocal methods, progress will follow which in a short time will advance the student a long way in the field of art and soon secure him the reputation of a true artist on the horn.' When Punto played in Prague a local review[38] remarked that 'his performance on this difficult instrument was always quite vocal', and Meifred underlined the relationship between vocal and horn music by arranging a selection of contemporary vocal studies for horn and piano in his 'Méthode'.[39]

Cadenzas

'The object of the cadenza', wrote Quantz,[40] 'is simply to take the listener by surprise at the end of the piece, and to leave behind a special impression in his heart.' Türk agrees, saying that they should include 'as much of the unexpected and surprising as can possibly be added',[41] but although 'novelty, with an abundance of ideas', is more appropriate than 'erudition', he also suggests that they offer an opportunity to present 'the most important parts of the whole composition in the form of a brief summary or in an extremely concise arrangement'.[42] The same view is held by Quantz, who advises that the cadenza should 'stem from the principal idea of the piece, and include a short repetition or imitation of its most pleasing phrases', and Türk says that 'intentionally added difficulties' are less acceptable than 'ideas which are scrupulously suited to the main character of the composition'.[43] Furthermore, the cadenza should modulate no further than the main part of the movement.[44] These recommendations clearly limit the scope for virtuoso display, but a number of surviving eighteenth-century cadenzas are made up entirely of elaborate scales and arpeggios and bear no resemblance to the main part of the movement.[45]

As regards length, Quantz takes the view that 'Vocal cadenzas, or cadenzas for a wind instrument must be so constituted that they can be performed in one breath', but adds that 'A string player can make them as long as he likes, if he is rich enough in inventiveness. Reasonable brevity, however, is more advantageous than vexing length.'[46] By the nineteenth century Dauprat felt that it was unreasonable to expect a wind player to perform in a single breath a cadenza 'which demonstrates all of one's skill and imagination',[47] and while most of the fourteen cadenzas which Meifred[48] includes in his tutor are 3–4 lines long, one – for a solo by Meifred himself – is six lines long. This is hardly excessive by comparison with the virtuoso offerings which were characteristic of contemporary violin and piano music, but is very long by comparison with the views voiced by Quantz.

Most writers take a pragmatic view of the need to improvise cadenzas. Quantz recognises that 'at times, if your thoughts are distracted it is not immediately possible to invent something new',[49] and suggests that 'the best expedient is to choose one of the most pleasing phrases which preceded it, and to fashion the cadenza from it. In this manner you compensate for any lack of inventiveness, but confirm the prevailing passion of the piece as well.' Dauprat takes a different stance:[50]

> These inspirations, these supposed improvisations, are often of long standing, having been completely thought out and elaborated in advance. But this fact is unimportant to the public as long as the cadenza pleases them. Think about your cadenza as much as you like. Copy it out with meticulous care. If it fits naturally into the piece and does not cause one to forget the main idea . . . and if, after this, it is skillfully played, and offers the listener expression, warmth, grace and lightness, you are sure of success.

He then quotes a large number of possible figurations. Türk points out that 'whether the player is making up the cadenza on the spur of the moment or has already sketched it beforehand is not going to be obvious to the listener', but decides that, as 'most of the audience pays more attention during the cadenza', improvising is 'too risky'. He also recommends that the player might try to deceive the audience, for, by changing the tempo and metre, he can make the cadenza sound 'more like a fantasia which has been fashioned out of an abundance of feeling than a methodically constructed composition'.[51]

Ornamentation

Ornamentation was a vitally important feature of musical style in the mid-eighteenth century, and as such is covered in considerable detail by C.P.E. Bach, Quantz and Leopold Mozart alike. In general, however, the horn repertoire from the period calls for little more than trills and appoggiaturas: the Concerto in D attributed to Haydn, Hob.VIId4 (see ch. 6) lends itself to some embellishment in the Adagio, as do Telemann's D major Concerto and Christoph Förster's Concerto no. 1 in E♭, but this is nothing by comparison with the range and number of embellishments which are appropriate in French harpsichord music. 'Some persons greatly abuse the use of extempore embellishments', wrote Quantz; ideally, they should be used 'like seasoning at a meal', for 'the rarest and most tasteful delicacies produce nausea if over-indulged'.[52] C.P.E. Bach took the same line: 'Regard them as spices which may ruin the best dish or gewgaws which may deface the most perfect building.'[53] To Quantz, the aim should be to play 'neither too simply nor too colourfully, always mixing simplicity and brilliance',[54] and to use a few, tasteful embellishments at appropriate points. Some may be extemporised in performance, but they should always be 'appropriate to the situation' and amenable to imitation by other players, although the opportunities for ornamentation are greatly reduced if there is more than one other player involved.

His view that ornaments should reflect 'the prevailing sentiment' of the work and never change its 'passion', is reiterated by Dauprat: the performer 'must not express anything that does not have a direct relation to the substance and form' of the composer's ideas. Embellishments can be added if they make the interpretation 'more energetic, more moving or more varied', but, as in the eighteenth century, they are not to be overdone: some performers 'would think their reputations compromised if they were to interpret a naïve passage with too much simplicity, if they did not insert what they call 'feeling' into a rondo that is full of gaiety, if they were to perform an Adagio without overloading it with notes, or an Agitato without altering the note values and exaggerating the dynamics'.[55]

Trills

All the eighteenth-century treatises agree that at this time trills should start on the note above the one which is written, but by the beginning of the nineteenth century this convention was changing, and in almost all of Dauprat's examples, they start on the note which is written, and then rise to the note above. This was soon to become standard and was explained by Hummel[56] as emphasising the main note rather than the subsidiary one. Leopold Mozart distinguishes between those whose first note is played at the same speed as the others, and those where it is treated like a long appoggiatura;[57] he also advocates the use of slow trills in sad pieces and faster ones in lively and spirited movements, and like C.P.E. Bach[58] identifies an uneven, 'dotted' trill known as the ribatutta, which, they agree, gradually accelerates into a conventional trill at the end of a cadenza (see Example 5.1).

Mozart likens a trill which is played too rapidly to the sound of a goat, 'unintelligible and bleating'[59] and Dauprat makes the same analogy,[60] but while Quantz says that in order to be 'genuinely beautiful' they 'must be played evenly' or at a 'uniform or moderate speed',[61] Mozart condones some acceleration, accompanied by a rise in dynamic from piano to forte. Quantz also concerns himself with the end of trills, suggesting a final turn or a two-note termination involving the note below the written one (see Example 5.2), but while Türk agrees that they should often have a two-note conclusion, not all of Leopold Mozart's examples close in this way.

Appoggiaturas

To C.P.E. Bach, appoggiaturas are among 'the most essential embellishments', for they 'enhance harmony as well as melody',[63] and Quantz says that they are a useful way of introducing dissonance – and hence interest – in otherwise wearisome consonant passages.[64] The same view is taken in the nineteenth century by Dauprat: 'It is by the tasteful use of various ornaments, such as dynamics and articulations, that variety can be introduced to melodies and other passages.'[65] Each of the authors attempts to define rules for the performance of notated accented and passing appoggiaturas, but Quantz feels that good taste needs to be the arbiter, for while

Example 5.1 Ribatutta as shown by C.P.E. Bach.

Example 5.2 Trill termination[62].

they can 'improve a piece where they are necessary', they can also 'mar it if used inappropriately'.[66] Their length and prominence varies according to their context, but they often last 'half the length of the main note'.[67] Dauprat sums up the problem facing the performer by pointing out that 'it is perhaps less difficult to choose dynamics, ornaments, and contrasts for this or that character, than to know how to combine them, to make them flow easily and appropriately, to use them without misusing them, and to do only what is required when it is required'.[68]

Articulation

To Dauprat articulation is 'an embellishment' which imbues a performance with 'life, colour and grace'.[69] In the past, he writes, 'passages grouped in fours had two slurred notes and two detached notes, while groups of triplets were played with the first two slurred and the third detached. These rules, it seemed, were never broken.'[70] By now, however, times had changed, and his tutor includes a quotation from one of Rosetti's double concertos both as it appears in print and with his own 'improved' articulation. He also paid the same attention to his own compositions, and, like Elgar after him, fills the solo lines of his concertos with an almost obsessive degree of detail.

Dotted rhythms

Among the particular issues which C.P.E. Bach addresses is the performance of dotted rhythms: both he[71] and Quantz[72] advise that the shorter note in a dotted phrase should be abbreviated so that a phrase like the one in Example 5.3 would be played as shown in Example 5.4. Bach adds that 'in

Example 5.3 Handel: Ouverture from The Royal Fireworks Music
(Opening).

Example 5.4.

Example 5.5.

Example 5.6.

general, the briskness of allegros is expressed by detached notes and the ten-
derness of adagios by broad, slurred notes',[73] and Mozart agrees, recom-
mending that dotted rhythms are given a lighter approach than is apparent
from the notation.[74] His intended reader, a violinist, can achieve this by
lifting the bow on dotted quaver-semiquaver rhythms; in horn playing terms
this means that the eighteenth century cliché shown in Example 5.5, is
played by sounding the notes for less than their full length, an interpretation
which most players find instinctive. The result, at the opening of Haydn
Symphony no. 47 or the opening of the Mozart horn concerto fragment
K370b is as shown in Example 5.6.

'Notes inégales'

'Notes inégales' were first used in seventeenth-century French
music and require pairs of quavers or semiquavers to be played unequally,

Example 5.7 Handel: an extract from 'Va tacito' ('Giulio Cesare').

Horn in F

Andante

usually with the emphasis on the first of the pair. An example is the horn obbligato in the aria, 'Va tacito' from Handel's *Giulio Cesare*, where the phrase shown in Example 5.7 is almost imperceptibly 'swung', with the first note of each pair lasting slightly longer than the second. The degree of inequality 'could vary from the barely perceptible to the equivalent of double dotting, according to the character of the piece and the taste of the performer',[75] but this requires flexibility and discretion. While there is a substantial body of evidence that notes inégales were the norm in French Baroque music (where horn parts are rare) their application elsewhere, and especially in the music of J.S. Bach, has been questioned in recent years. It would certainly be as wrong to play all equal quavers as dotted rhythms as it would be to play them all with rigid rhythmic precision.

6   Case studies

Bach: Quoniam from Mass in B minor, BWV 232

The bass aria in which Bach sets the words, 'Quoniam tu solus sanctus, tu solus dominus, tu solus altissimus'[1] in the Mass in B minor is one of the most distinctive obbligatos in the solo horn repertoire. On the few occasions when the horn plays an obbligato in the first half of the eighteenth century, its line is usually less complex than this, and it is most unusual for it to be the only treble clef instrument in the ensemble. Its high tessitura is unsurprising, for the Baroque horn could not play melodically anywhere else, but like the voice, the accompanying bassoons and the bass line, the horn has its own exclusive melodic material which it does not share with anyone else. Furthermore, as he does not play anywhere else in the Mass, the horn player has to sit in the orchestra for about fifty minutes, thinking of both the vertiginous opening leap up to written top C (the sixteenth harmonic of the natural horn pitched in D; see Example 6.1) and the torrents of semiquavers which follow. The long wait causes anguish even when the player has the assistance of an F-alto valve horn; pity the natural horn player whose conductor also asks him to stand up to play it!

Although Bach assembled the Mass in about 1749, much of it dates from earlier in his career and the Quoniam was among the parts of the Gloria which were composed for the installation of the Elector of Saxony at Dresden in 1733.[2] If it was performed at this date, the horn obbligato would probably have been played by Johann or Andreas Schindler,[3] but when Spitta saw the surviving orchestral parts in 1873 they were in such pristine condition that he thought that they may never have been used. If not, one of the Quoniam's earliest performances took place in May 1838 at the English première of parts of the Gloria and Credo. The result was not a success: 'The passages for the horn were next to impracticable' wrote, *The Musical World*; 'the selection was slaughtered, soli players retiring in dismay, and leaving Mr Knyvett to play their parts on the organ'.[4]

Example 6.1 Bach: Mass in B Minor, BWV 232. Opening of the Quoniam.

Horn in D

It is unlikely that Bach expected the part to cause so much trouble. At home in Leipzig, the horn part would conventionally have been played by a trumpeter, who would not have found its tessitura as awesome as it appears to the horn player today. He would also have had other work to do earlier in the Mass, and so would not have had to wait so long to play. It is, therefore, not outside the spirit of eighteenth-century performance practice for the modern performer to warm up, by agreement with the conductor, by playing the third trumpet part discreetly during the earlier movements. A copy of the vocal score reduces the feeling of loneliness, and, if you sit near the chamber organ, you will be able to hear the only other high-pitched frequencies in the ensemble. Finally, check that the edition is not grotesquely over-edited; Bärenreiter's is mostly fine, but beware bar 60 where the trill should be over the third beat, not the second.

A more specific problem lies in the range of notes in the obbligato line. Eighteenth-century trumpeters may well have dealt with the naturally out-of-tune eleventh and thirteenth harmonics by bending them to the right pitch, but the third line B which appears in bar 40 is completely outside the harmonic series. The same note appears elsewhere in a number of trumpet works, including 'Jauchzet Gott in allen Landen' BWV 51 (last movement, bar 9) and in the horn line of Brandenburg Concerto no. 1, BWV 1046 (first movement, bar 33), four times in the first movement of the cantata, 'Wie schön leuchtet der Morgenstern', BWV1, (1725) and twice, alongside an equally unlikely 3rd space C♯, in the chorale which closes the fourth cantata of the *Christmas Oratorio* BWV 248. Its appearance in trumpet parts need not preclude the possibility of hand stopping, for Bach's favourite player, Gottfried Reiche, owned a coiled instrument which probably responded to the use of fingers in the bell. Similarly, although 'Wie schön leuchtet', the Quoniam, and BWV 248 long predate Hampel, having been composed in 1725, 1733 and 1734 respectively, the rudiments of hand stopping had been known sixty miles away in Dresden, since 1717.[5] Modern horn players who prefer not to qualify the tuning of their instrument by lipping or hand stopping do have the option of using an instrument equipped with nodal vents, but there is no historical precedent for doing so.

Haydn: Concerto in D (Hob. viid: 3) and attrib. Haydn: Concerto in D (Hob. viid: 4)

The horn appears frequently in Haydn's scores, and while his symphonies include some of the most interesting parts for the eighteenth-century instrument, he also wrote a number of concertos for it to play. The incipits of Hob. viid: 1 for solo horn in D major and Hob. viid: 2 in E♭ for two horns, appear in his catalogue, but while the scores of these are now lost, Hob. viid: 3, in D major, survives today as his concerto 'no. 1'. This is not in the catalogue but is clearly authentic, for the copy in Vienna's Gesellschaft der Musikfreunde[6] is in Haydn's handwriting, and is signed 'Giuseppe Haydn [1]762'. Another work for two horns in E♭ is published by Ka-We, but although it is generally accepted that the words 'par Michael Heiden' are later additions to the only known source,[7] there is no good reason for attributing it to Joseph as the opening is not the same as the incipit of Hob. viid: 2. Instead, it is more likely to be the work of Antonio Rosetti or one of his colleagues in the court orchestra at Oettingen-Wallerstein. Finally, the D major concerto, Hob. viid: 4, is widely known today as Haydn's 'Concerto no. 2' and is published as such by both Breitkopf & Härtel and Boosey & Hawkes. It was first listed by Breitkopf in 1781,[8] but it is not included in Haydn's catalogue and a copy which is said to have survived in Breitkopf's Leipzig archive was presumably destroyed during the second world war. The only remaining source is therefore a set of parts whose title page reads, 'Concerto a 5. Corno Secondo Principale, Violino Primo, e Secondo, Viola e Basso', and which came to light in a library in Zittau.[9] It is easy to see how this might be read as 'Concerto no. 2', but it was clearly intended for 'second' – i.e. low – horn accompanied by a chamber group made up of two violins, viola, cello, and, perhaps, unfigured continuo. Its unsophisticated form, and its isolation in Zittau, 300 miles from Esterházy, cast doubt over its authorship, and as Haydn was a frequent target for unscrupulous publishers, the words 'Del Signore Haÿden' on the title page need not be taken too seriously.

Example 6.2 Haydn: Concerto in D (Hob.VIId: 3), 2nd movement.

Horn in D

The concerto Hob. VIId: 3 dates from 1762, when Haydn was new to the Esterházy Court and was working hard to impress his colleagues with his music. It is therefore generally assumed that he intended the concerto for one of them to play, and Haydn's extremely imaginative use of the horn's lowest register in the Adagio makes the second horn player, Thaddäus Steinmüller, a likely candidate (see Example 6.2). Alternatively, Haydn may have written the concerto as a present for the christening, on 3 July 1762, of the daughter of Joseph Leutgeb. The two families were close enough for Haydn's wife to become the baby's godmother, and it has been suggested that in noting 'written in my sleep', on the manuscript, Haydn meant that he composed it after he had finished work for the day. A third possibility is that he wrote it in anticipation of a visit by Leutgeb to Esterházy: the court's records mention 'the chamber hunting horn player Joseph Leitgeb, engaged by H.S.H. at the beginning of the month of February [1763]' but then add that he 'was dismissed at the end of the said month'.[10] The obvious interpretation of this entry is that Leutgeb was appointed and immediately sacked, but it is equally possible that he was engaged as a soloist on a very short contract for a particular event.

Whatever the identity of Haydn's player, there can be no doubt of his ability. As well as descending to the 2nd harmonic, the concerto climbs repeatedly to the sixteenth harmonic (top C), and each movement includes a top D (eighteenth harmonic). The horn part includes relatively few indications of articulation, but as the first violin parts are full of markings the players need to liaise closely, and it may help to bear in mind Geminiani's advice to harpsichordists concerning the performance of acciaccaturas: 'touch the key lightly, and quit it with a Spring, as if it were Fire'.[11] Stopped notes appear less frequently than in early nineteenth-century works, but Haydn uses them with assurance, and the greatest problem is his frequent use of the 13th harmonic (A above the stave). This note was always considered difficult,[12] but Haydn compounds the problem by including it in two trills, once with the B above (1st movement, bar 59) and once with the G below (1st movement, bar 111). His treatment of modulation is imaginative, for the Adagio opens in A major (the dominant of the D crook) before modulating to E major (the supertonic) and then uses bottom C (sounding D) as the fourth degree of the tonic of the movement when the main theme is repeated (see Example 6.2).

In contrast, Hob. viid: 4 relies almost exclusively on open notes. The outer movements show some understanding of sonata form, but the slow movement stays in B minor or D, its relative major, throughout. The composer uses the lowest harmonics, but these are reached by sudden awkward leaps, and he seems ill at ease with the third movement cadenza, which, in its original form,[13] is preceded by a root position D major chord and an awkward silence. Today, this quirky approach is usually cut so that the cadenza follows the conventional second inversion chord, but this does not disguise the relative lack of sophistication in the score in general, and it is reasonable to conclude that Hob. viid: 4 is really by an earlier composer whose ideas did not yet quite embrace Classicism. A number of pointers suggest that it may instead be the work of a Dresden composer: the parts emerged in Zittau, just forty miles to the east of the city, and its melodic leaps and rudimentary use of hand stopping recall a concerto in Eb by Rheinhardt (see Examples 6.3 and 6.4).[14] It also bears stylistic similarities both to a concerto attributed to Hampel,[15] and to a set of horn duets by Haudek (see Example 6.5).[16] If these suppositions are correct, Hob. viid: 4 can be freed from direct comparisons with Hob. viid: 3, and emerge, not as a poor relation, but as a delightful piece of pre-Classical writing.

Example 6.3 Attrib. Haydn, Concerto in D (Hob. VIId: 4), 1st movement.

Horn in D

Example 6.4 Reinhardt: Concerto in E♭, 1st movement.

Horn in E flat

Example 6.5 Karl Haudek: Duet No. 10 from 28 'Duetts'.

Mozart: Concerto in E♭, K495

Although the finale of Mozart's horn concerto in E♭, K495, is the best known of all horn solos today, the details surrounding its composition are lost. Mozart noted in his 'Verzeichnüss' or little catalogue, that it was written for Joseph Leutgeb and that he finished it on 26 June 1786, but we cannot be sure of the date of its first performance, or, in the absence of any orchestral parts, how many strings accompanied it; the only hint we have is that in 1782 the Viennese court orchestra had twelve violins, four violas, three cellos and three basses.[17] The manuscript[18] is in the Pierpont Morgan Library, New York, but is far from complete, for while the second movement survives from bar 22 onwards, the whole of the first movement and the first 139 of the 217 bars of the rondo are lost. Any performing edition therefore has to be derived from printed editions which were published after Mozart's death, but these are sometimes demonstrably inaccurate: in the finale, for example, bars 105–8 are repeated in the most reliable early edition, but were then inexplicably omitted by every later editor until the publication of Bärenreiter's New Mozart Edition in 1987.[20]

Nor do we have any explanation of Mozart's eccentric use of of red, blue, black and green inks in the manuscript. One unlikely explanation is that they represent coded instructions on dynamics,[21] but it is more probable that Mozart included them simply to amuse himself or Leutgeb. A third possibility is that he used the inks to give the score a festive appearance. He was hard at work on *The Marriage of Figaro* early in 1786, when Leutgeb married for the second time, but he started work on K495 shortly after the opera's first performance on 1 May. Might the brightly coloured score have been written as a belated wedding present?

The earliest printed edition of K495 was published as 'Third Concerto, op. 106', by Johann André in Offenbach in 1802, but is 43 bars shorter than a second version which followed from Vienna's 'Contore delle arti e d'industria' on 31 August 1803. André also omits all the low Gs and avoids most of the high Cs which feature in the Viennese edition, and the position is further confused by the survival in Prague of a copyist's manuscript[22] which has a further 13 bars of orchestral tutti. However, the recent revision of the dates traditionally associated with the composition of Mozart's horn concertos[23] sheds light on his thinking, and helps to explain the differences between the printed editions of K495.

Mozart started writing horn concertos in 1781 with the two incomplete movements, K370b and the 'Concert Rondo' K371. These were followed, in 1783, by the Concerto K417 which was previously known as 'No. 2' and in 1785/6 by the first 91 bars of a Concerto in E, K494a. The old 'No. 4', K495, came later in 1786, and while the precise date of 'No. 3' K447, is unclear, some of the manuscript is written on the same batch of paper as *Don Giovanni* which was composed in 1787. Finally comes K412, the concerto which is traditionally called 'No. 1', but which Mozart had not finished at the time of his death.

This reordering highlights the way in which the concertos become gradually less taxing with time. K417 and K495 are both in E♭, and offered Leutgeb every opportunity to demonstrate the sound which 'never ceases to amaze the connoisseur',[24] and his ability to play athletic runs up to the sixteenth harmonic (top C). K447 is also in E♭, but avoids the highest notes of the first two complete concertos, and Mozart's decision to move down a semitone to D in K412 probably reflects the fact that by 1791 Leutgeb was fifty-nine years old. Furthermore, in the first movement the solo line falls within a minor ninth, and by the time Süssmayr completed the Rondo in 1792, he felt it necessary to remove the lowest of the original notes to contain the horn part within a single octave. Whether Mozart's decision to abandon the Concerto K494a had anything to do with Leutgeb's ability in the higher key is not clear – like K370b and K371, it cannot be linked to him with absolute certainty – but the concertos' general trend towards a reduced technical requirement, and the fact that Leutgeb retired later in 1792, suggest that André's edition of K495 may be a simplified version which was made to accommodate Leutgeb's failing lip. As the extra bars in the copyist's manuscript cannot be authenticated, the 'Contore delle arti' version is, therefore, the best in terms of notes, but as the string articulation is more convincing in André's edition, it is advisable to consult both before making a performing edition.

Mozart's understanding of hand horn writing is as clear from the notes he avoids as from the way he uses others. The complete absence of 1st space F, and the D and C♯ above middle C, cannot be coincidental, for although they appear in nineteenth-century tutors, they are difficult to play musically. Conversely, his melodic lines lie well on the instrument, and in the hands of a skilled player the phrase shown in Example 6.6 can be played with a fairly

Example 6.6 Mozart: Concerto in E♭, K495, 1st movement, bars 36–40.

Horn in E flat

constant tone colour. The half-stopped F in bar 37 has two open notes on either side, and, played carefully, will merely sound a little veiled. The B and A have to be stopped, but as the first B follows a C it is easy make it sound a little quieter, and the last two quavers will merge in well if they are not forced. The only other heavily stopped note, the B on the 3rd beat of bar 39, can be played quite forcefully as it appears on a strong beat; any sizzle will add colour to the phrase.

Mozart's understanding of stopped notes is so good that it allows him to use them to underline his melodic intentions. See, for example, bars 98 and 106, where he moves down from a half stopped A to a heavily stopped G♯: (see Example 6.7) The G♯ is quite a difficult note, but approached in this way it is almost impossible to play badly, and will inevitably produce the feminine ending which Mozart wants. For the same reason, bars 102–4 are easier to play musically on the hand horn than on the valve horn (see Example 6.8), where the snarling caused by the need to stop F, D♯ and C♯ is in keeping with the mood of the chromatic scale, and, because the stopped B in bar 104 is approached from the C above, it is easy to play gently and stylishly. Indeed, the construction of the phrase means that the hand horn player automatically produces a feminine ending, even though the stopped note falls on a strong beat.

The slow movement is clearly designed to display Leutgeb's singing tone. The only serious textual problem concerns the orchestral parts in bars 46–9, where repeat signs have been added in the first violin part of the autograph score. Whether this alteration originates with Mozart is not known, and it is rarely performed today, but it is an option in Bärenreiter's New Mozart Edition, and the effect is certainly musical.

The galloping rhythm of the 6/8 finale recalls the horn's ancestry on the

Example 6.7 Mozart: Concerto in E♭, K495, 1st movement, bars 98 and 106.

Horn in E flat

Example 6.8 Mozart: Concerto in E♭, K495, 1st movement, bars102–4.

Horn in E flat
Allegro maestoso

hunting field and has since become a cliché, but it was unknown in Baroque horn writing and made some of its first appearances in the concertos and wind partitas which Antonio Rosetti wrote from the 1770s onwards.

Beethoven: Sonata in F, op 17

Although Beethoven composed only one sonata for horn, he already had considerable understanding of the instrument, both as a result of his youthful friendship with Nikolaus Simrock and from his experience of composing the Sextet for two horns and strings, op. 81b, in 1795. Simrock is best known today as Beethoven's publisher in Bonn, but he had originally been a horn player and gave the composer a considerable amount of advice on the instrument's potential and limitations. The success of his lessons is shown by the score of the Sextet, for, while Beethoven taxes both horn players to their limits, he takes into account the distinction between cor alto and cor basse parts, taking the first horn flying up to the eighteenth harmonic while rattling arpeggios take the second horn down to the lowest notes it can play. 'The pupil has given the master many a hard nut to crack', joked Simrock when Beethoven sent him the manuscript for publication in 1810.[25]

Ferdinand Ries[26] records that although Beethoven, his teacher, undertook

Example 6.9 Beethoven: Sonata in F, Op. 17, 1st movement, bars 160–2.

to write a sonata which he could play with Punto at a concert in Vienna on 18 April 1800, he had not started the score 24 hours before the event. In fact, he had sketched the slow movement some months before and Punto must have had a complete horn part in time for the performance, but Beethoven probably improvised from a draft of the piano part, finalising it in time for the second performance, which he gave with Punto in Budapest on May 7.

No earlier work for horn and piano survives – Franz Süssmayr's sketches for a sonata[27] are woefully incomplete – and while the standard of the first performance was probably high, its sheer novelty probably also played a part in the audience's demand for an immediate encore.[28] Earlier composers' neglect of the pairing is easy to understand, for the instruments were far from natural partners, and the problem of achieving a satisfactory balance between a natural horn and a five-octave Viennese fortepiano is one of the main challenges for 'authentic' performances today. Beethoven's preference for pianos by the Stein family is well known,[29] and Punto played a silver Raoux cor solo which had been made for him in about 1780,[30] but it would be just as appropriate to use an instrument built along the same lines as Louis Dauprat's brass Raoux cor solo with silver mounts.[31]

The sonata clearly reflects Punto's brilliance as a cor basse, for it does not rise above the 12th harmonic (G at the top of the stave) and all three movements make substantial use of the notes below the stave. The sturdy descent to low C which opens the work by is absolutely characteristic of such parts, and both the first and third movements are full of arpeggios, the natural vehicle for a low horn player's virtuosity. Second horn players would also take a particular delight in performing the factitious low G in bar 161 (see Example 6.9). As it is relatively easy to lip the 2nd harmonic (the C) down to

Example 6.10 Beethoven: Sextet, Op. 81b, Rondo, bars 196–200.

Example 6.11 Beethoven: Symphony no. 9 in D minor, Op. 125, 3rd movement, bars 96–7.

Example 6.12 H. Domnich: Méthode de Premier et de Seconde Cor, p. 55.

a G, or even an F♯, the fact that the G is not in the harmonic series is unimportant, and Beethoven uses the same technique to get the second horn down a chromatic scale from C to G in the Sextet (see Example 6.10). A third example of a factitious G occurs as part of the extraordinary fourth horn solo in bars 83–141 of the second movement of the 9th Symphony. This section is typical of cor basse writing, and the famous unaccompanied scale in bar 96 recalls a passage in Domnich's hand horn tutor (see Examples 6.11 and 6.12). It is said that at the first performance of the symphony, on 7 May 1824, the fourth horn part was played by Domnich's pupil, Eduard Lewy. While it would certainly not have caused him any difficulty on the hand horn, there is a remote possibility that he played it on an early valve horn, for only three years later he delighted 'a numerous audience' in Strasburg 'by his admirable performance on the instrument.'[32]

Example 6.13 Beethoven: Sonata in F, Op. 17, 1st movement, bars 96–8.

Example 6.14 Beethoven: Sonata in F, Op. 17, 1st movement, bar 14.

Example 6.15 Beethoven: Sonata in F, Op. 17, 1st movement, bar 119.

Despite his obvious confidence with cor basse writing, however, Beethoven has less success in using the horn to his advantage than Mozart. His choice of the shorter and brighter F crook magnifies the difference in tone quality between open and stopped notes, and while he stays below the 13th harmonic which so often causes difficulty in Mozart's work, it is more difficult to avoid sudden, inappropriate changes in tone colour in his melodic lines. Bars 96–8 from the first movement of the Sonata often sound particularly unmusical on a hand horn (see Example 6.13), as between the asterisks all but the last of the off beats are open, and all the main beat notes are stopped. The stopped sounds do little to enhance the melody, and just as the ear is adjusting, bar 98 begins with an open note, so most players will need to work hard to even out the sound. By way of compensation, however, you may enjoy the prospect of inserting a short cadenza under the pause in bar 131 of the finale: few players take this opportunity, but to do so would match the short piano cadenza which is written at the end of the slow movement.

Finally, you will need to take a view about the discrepancy between bar 14 of the exposition and bar 119 of the recapitulation. Did Beethoven intend the two to be different, or is this a printer's error which has been replicated ever since? (See Examples 6.14 and 6.15).

Schubert: Auf dem Strom D943

On 26 March 1828, Franz Schubert presented the first and last concert which he devoted exclusively to his own work. The programme opened with the first movement of his G major string quartet, D887, and finished with the 'Schlachtgesang' ('Battlesong'), D912, for male voices. Fifth in the programme was an extended new setting of Rellstab's poem, 'Auf dem Strom' ('On the River'), which was performed by the tenor Ludwig Tietze and the horn player Joseph Rudolph Lewy, with Schubert himself at the piano.[33]

Lewy had been in Vienna since he joined his older brother, Eduard Constantin, in the horn section at the Imperial Opera in 1822. When he met Schubert is unclear, but on Sunday 22 April 1827 he was joined in the Great Hall of the Gesellschaft der Musikfreunde by four male singers and three other horn players – his brother Eduard, Johann Nepomuk Janatka, and R. Leeser – to give the first performance of Schubert's 'Nachtgesang im Walde'.[34] The fourth horn part in this work clearly requires a valve horn, and the passage which appears between bars 129–34 and bars 143–8 of 'Auf dem Strom' is similarly impractical without valves (see Example 6.16).

The problem is that while all of these notes are available to a hand horn player, they are strangely unidiomatic in this configuration, and bar 132 is virtually impossible to play convincingly. Indeed, how Lewy played these passages depends on the number of valves he used: one of the brothers is said to have owned a 3-valve horn as early as 1825,[35] but it is still possible that in 1828 Joseph had only two, and therefore had to play the G♯ in bar 131 either by lipping it up from the open note below, or by depressing both valves and playing it as a stopped note. Those who still played the hand horn, would, however, have found the passages more difficult, and Schubert probably had

Example 6.16   Schubert: 'Auf dem Strom' D943, bars 129–34.

this in mind when he gave the horn the support of the voice doubling it at the octave.

Lewy left Vienna to tour Europe in 1834, but settled in Dresden in 1837, and as principal horn in the city's Hofkapelle may have had some influence over the young Wagner. In 1841, when he met Berlioz, he played 'a cylinder or rotary valve horn' which was now almost certainly equipped with three valves,[36] and by 1849 Lewy had impressed Schumann sufficiently for the composer to recommend his '12 studies for chromatic horn and natural horn' to Breitkopf and Härtel. 'What I have seen of them', he wrote, 'seems to me good and practical, as cannot but be expected from one who has made a lifelong study of his instrument.'[37] Some of Lewy's studies offer proof of the contemporary German practice of combining hand and valve horn techniques, for their transpositions change so frequently that the player is obliged to treat the valves as a way of making a quick change of crook.

Most modern editions of 'Auf dem Strom' follow the first printed edition, which was published by Leidesdorf in Vienna in 1829, but there are over 150 differences between this and Schubert's rather scrappy autograph manuscript which survives in Harvard University Library.[38] Many reflect a careless approach to printing slurs and, as is common among Schubert's early publishers, a tendency to misread his rather exaggerated accent markings as diminuendi. There are many other more serious discrepancies, however: at the beginning of bar 17, for example, Schubert himself wrote only a minim on C; the D appoggiatura is apparently an invention by the publisher. On several occasions the rhythm of the horn part should really match the vocal line: in bars 40, 78 and 148 the horn should have minims, not crotchets, and in bars 55, 57, 69 and 71 its four equal quavers should really be in dotted quaver-semiquaver rhythm. Perhaps the most serious of the errors occurs, however, in bars 149–50, where, in the printed editions, the voice and horn are silent and the piano plays only an accompaniment figure. There is, therefore, no melody, although in a similar passage which starts at bar 79, the tune appears in the piano part. A cursory glance at the manuscript solves the problem: when Schubert first wrote bars 149–50, he wrote the melody in the horn line, and although the printer noticed that he subsequently crossed it out, he did not understand that, in doing so, the composer moved it to the piano part (see Example 6.17).

If 'Auf dem Strom' were a minor work, such discrepancies would perhaps have only academic value. We now know, however,[39] that it was probably written as a tribute to Beethoven, whose death fell exactly a year before the first performance. Schubert, who greatly admired Beethoven and had been a torch-bearer at his funeral, can scarcely have overlooked the anniversary and his apparent quotations in verses 2 and 4 of the funeral march from the *Eroica* Symphony would therefore be significant even if Beethoven had not dedicated the symphony 'to the memory of a great man' (see Examples 6.18 and 6.19).

Following the composition of 'Auf dem Strom', songs with horn obbligato were written by a number of others including Schubert's friends, Franz, Ignaz and Vinzenz Lachner. Heinrich Proch was the most prolific of the Viennese composers to write in the genre, but his colleague Conradin Kreutzer wrote 'Das Mühlrad' and Nicolai produced 'Die Träne' and the 'Variazioni Concertanti' on a favourite melody from *La Sonnambula*. Works by visitors to the city include *L'amor funesto* by Donizetti and Berlioz's *Le jeune Pâtre Breton* which were published in Vienna by Mechetti in 1844 and 1845 respectively. It is likely that the key to the interest in the genre lies in a letter which Mendelssohn sent to his sister, Rebecka, on 22 August 1830. The composer complains that the first of three interruptions to his train of thought came in the form of a visit from 'Levy, the Waldhorn player, who ordered a serenade for voice and horn which he wants to bugle beneath the windows of some beautiful young lady . . .'[40] No song with horn obbligato by Mendelssohn survives, but as Joseph Lewy left Vienna for a series of concert tours in 1834, and the city's string of works for voice, horn and piano stops in 1846, the year of Eduard Lewy's death, it is likely that it was the older of the two brothers who was responsible for this local interest in an otherwise unlikely combination of timbres.

Example 6.17 Schubert: 'Auf dem Strom' D943, bars 149–52. The large notes are present in Schubert's manuscript but are absent from most published editions. The vocal line, which rests throughout the extract, has been omitted.

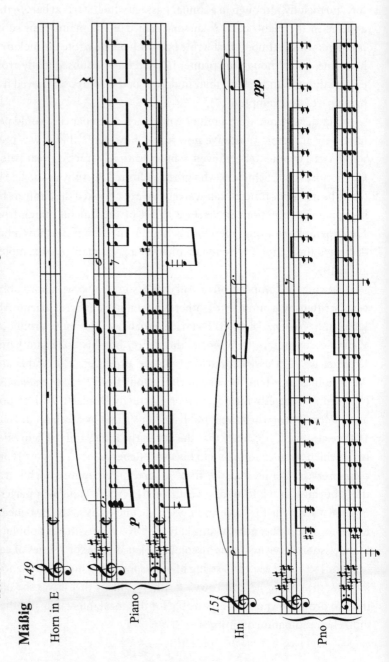

Example 6.18 Schubert: 'Auf dem Strom' D943, bars 64–8.

Voice

Example 6.19 Beethoven: Symphony no. 3 in E♭, Op. 55, 2nd movement: Marcia funebre, bars 1–4.

Violin 1

Schumann: Adagio and Allegro in A♭, op 70

The 'Adagio and Allegro' is the first horn solo to reflect the new spirit of Romanticism in music, and is one of a number of works which Schumann wrote for the instrument in 1849: composed between 14th and 17th February, it was followed between 18th and 20th by the short score of the *Conzertstück* op. 86, for four horns and orchestra,[41] and, later in the year, by the '5 Hunting Songs' op. 137, for male voices and horn quartet. The main attraction seems to have been the horn's sound, for he opened up its bottom register to an even greater degree than Haydn, and made a point of writing seamless, tonally free-ranging lines throughout its range. He was also, however, at the mercy of his precarious mental state, and, as the political situation in Dresden worsened, was composing frenziedly: the *Phantasiestücke* op. 73, for clarinet and piano date from 11th and 12th February, and the orchestration of the *Conzertstück* was complete within three weeks. 'I have been very busy', he wrote to Ferdinand Hiller. 'It is just as if the outward storms drive me in on myself, for only in my work have I found compensation for the terrible storm which burst upon me from the outside.'[42]

Schumann clearly saw parallels between himself and Johannes Kreisler, the fictional Kapellmeister who appears in the writing of E.T.A. Hoffmann, and whose mental instability and implied madness was dangerously close to his own experience. Many of Schumann's most inspired chamber works and songs were written in a state of impetuous anxiety, so it was easy for him to understand Kreisler, who would 'compose at night in extreme excitation, waking his friend whose room was nearby to play compositions which he had written with incredible speed in this inspired state of mind. He would shed tears of joy over his success, holding himself to be the luckiest of men. But the next day the splendid composition would be in the fire.'[43] Neither Kreisler nor Schumann was helped by the spirit of the times, for the discipline and structure which had characterised the late eighteenth century had by now been replaced by a culture which indulged unrestrained emotion and temperament, and, indeed, the 'Adagio and Allegro' was first known as 'Romance and Allegro'.[44]

Clara Schumann played through the score within two weeks of its composition and commented that it was 'just the sort of piece that I like, brilliant, fresh and passionate'[45] but she does not comment on the success of the contribution made by her otherwise forgotten horn player, Schlitterlau. It is difficult to believe that he found it easy: here, for the first time is the sound which was to become inextricably associated with the Romantic horn, and while the opening of the Allegro recalls the spirit and shape of hand horn music, it soon becomes impractical without valves, and Schumann's use of B major – 6 sharps for the horn in F – in the central 'Etwas Ruhiger' would have been unthinkable just a few years earlier (see Example 6.20). Nor does he accommodate horn players' need to breathe or to rest their lip, and although he certainly knew Joseph Lewy, he shows no sign of understanding the problems which players encounter with stamina. Schlitterlau probably also had difficulties with the manuscript, in which Schumann encapsulates his lack of interest in traditional horn technique and conventions by writing the solo part an octave above concert pitch in the score.

More is known about the première of the formidably difficult *Conzertstück*, on 25 February 1850 at the Leipzig Gewandhaus, when the first horn, Eduard Pohle, is said to have panicked and abandoned his valve horn in favour of his tried and tested hand horn.[46] While this seems barely credible today, hand horn players were accustomed to overcoming fearsome problems, and in 1843 Leipzig was said by Berlioz to be the only German city

Example 6.20 Schumann: Adagio and Allegro, Op. 70, bars 120–38.

Horn in F

to resist the use of valves.[47] This view is substantiated by a drawing of Pohle holding a hand horn in 1845.[48]

Schumann's disinterest in the horn's traditional characteristics also meant that he was quite happy to sanction an arrangement of the *Conzertstück* for piano and orchestra, and to offer the 'Adagio and Allegro' in splendid alternative versions for cello, violin, or viola. The Mozart horn concertos are unimaginable on the cello, and yet neither arrangement of Schumann's works sounds like a piece which was originally intended for horn, and Peter Landgren's transcription for horn of the clarinet *Phantasiestücke*, op. 73,[49] sounds extremely convincing. It is ironic that, by becoming fully chromatic, the horn lost the distinctive style which had once been one of its virtues.

Brahms: Trio in E♭, op. 40

Brahms' writing for brass is often said to been influenced by his experience of learning the hand horn as a boy, for almost every note which he scored for trumpets or horns could, in theory, be played on instruments without valves. His adult preference for the natural horn also reflected, however, his serious interest in the music of the past: while Wagner was developing theories about 'the artwork of the future', Brahms was assidu-

Example 6.21 Brahms: Academic Festival Overture, Op. 80, bars 258–69.

ously preparing scholarly editions of French Baroque music, making a collection which included autograph manuscripts by Mozart and Schubert, and building a circle of friends which included some of the most eminent musicologists of the age. He openly acknowledged both Handel and Haydn in sets of variations, and his particular affection for the music of Bach is clear from his choral preludes for organ, his use of cantata no. 150 as the basis of the finale of the fourth symphony, and the magnificent fugal writing in the *German Requiem*.

Bach had also enjoyed the challenge of an intellectual puzzle, and in works like *The Art of Fugue* was testing his ability to write music which fulfilled a number of preconceived criteria. Richard Merewether suggests that, in writing for the hand horn long after most German professional players had taken to valves, Brahms was taking a similarly cerebral approach, and his use of the term 'gestopft' to show which notes are to be stopped in the first edition of the Academic Festival Overture[50] (see Example 6.21) implies that in 1880 he accepted, and wanted to exploit, the likelihood that the work would usually now be played with valves.

Little is known about the first performance of the Horn Trio, which took place in Zurich on 28 November 1865 with Brahms at the piano and a player named Glass on the horn.[51] By now, valve horns were well established in

German profesional circles, but we can infer from a letter which Brahms sent to his friend Albert Dietrich that Segisser, first horn in the Karlsruhe opera, played the hand horn when he gave the second performance in the city on 7 December.[52] Dietrich had voiced an interest in organising a further performance, and Brahms advised that, 'Your horn player will do me a great favour if, like the Karlsruhe man, he practises the natural horn for some weeks beforehand and plays it on that.'[53] Another letter gives more detail: 'The stopped notes mean that the horn player has to play softly. If he doesn't do this, the piano and violin don't have to adapt their sound to his, and the tone is rough from the outset.'[54] Dietrich complied, and when Brahms arrived in Oldenburg to play the piano in his performance on 10 January 1866, the horn player Westermann was ready with his natural horn.

Brahms could only influence the choice of instrument when he was personally involved in the performance, however, and when Friedrich Gumbert, the distinguished section leader at the Gewandhaus, played the Trio on 15 December 1866, the pianist, Clara Schumann, recorded that 'he couldn't be persuaded to use a natural horn'. Instead, his preferred choice of instrument was almost certainly the wide bore terminally crooked rotary valve horn which the Leipzig maker, J. C. G. Penzel[55] marketed as the 'Gumbert-Modell' from about 1875. By now, professionals in southern Germany, such as Franz Strauss, were beginning to rely on the B♭ alto crook,[56] but Gumbert preferred to use this only for difficult entries, and probably played the Trio on an E♭ crook. Clara was delighted with the 'splendid' result, adding 'I don't think he cracked a single note, and that says a great deal'.[57] Gumbert had a considerable influence on the development of horn playing, first through his nephew, Edmund Gumpert, who teamed up with Eduard Kruspe to design the first double horn, and, in the twentieth century, through his pupils, Anton Horner, Max Pottag and Max Hess, who played an important part in introducing wide-bore instruments to America.

Another notable early performance of the Trio was given in Basle on 26 March 1867, when the horn part was played by the young Hans Richter.[58] Richter was already developing a reputation as a conductor, but having studied with Eduard Lewy's son, Richard, at the Vienna Conservatoire, and having played at the Kärntnertor Theatre from 1862–6,[59] he remained very

Example 6.22 Brahms: Trio in E♭, Op. 40, 3rd movement, bars 59–61.

Horn in E flat

Example 6.23 Brahms: Trio in E♭, Op. 40, 3rd movement, bars 65–7.

Horn in E flat

much a product of the city's school of horn playing. It is therefore possible that in the first five years of its life Brahms' Trio was performed variously on natural, rotary valved, and Vienna horns. It was first published by Simrock in 1866, and a comparison with Brahms' autograph manuscript[60] reveals that, apart from some obvious misprints, their subsequent miniature score is an accurate reflection of his intentions. The Peters edition raises a possible area of confusion by claiming as its source the 'second edition' of 1891, but there are no grounds for thinking that Brahms made any changes to the score after the publication of the first edition, and in fact the Peters edition is identical with earlier versions.

That Brahms can be as sensitive to the horn as any of his predecessors is shown towards the end of the third movement of the Trio. First, the predominantly open note phrase shown in Example 6.22, is answered exquisitely by an even quieter line, in which the A♮ and F♯ are gently veiled half-stopped notes (Example 6.23). Then, in the climax, he takes full advantage of the potential of D♭, F and A♭ to snarl when forced, and after writing glorious ringing open notes in descending octaves, makes it as easy as possible to play the difficult factitious F (see Example 6.24). There are certainly occasional moments elsewhere, such as the opening of the trio in the second movement, where Brahms pushes hand horn technique to its very limits, and it is

Example 6.24 Brahms: Trio in E♭, Op. 40, 3rd movement, bars 73–7.

Example 6.25 Brahms: Trio in E♭, Op. 40, 2nd movement, bars 287–98.

Example 6.26 Brahms: Trio in E♭, Op. 40, Finale, bars 62–7.

easy to understand from the passage in Example 6.25 why Gumbert preferred valves but most of the finale is very sensitive to the hand horn. A well-developed technique is needed for, say, bars 61–7 (see Example 6.26), but the coda avoids stopped notes almost completely, and the horn rings out to bring the work to a thrilling close.

Notes

1 Introduction

1. *Musical Directory, Annual and Almanack,* 58th Annual Issue (London: Rudall, Carte and Co., 1910), pp. 102 and 117.
2. For a fuller account of the history of the Early Music Movement, see: Colin Lawson and Robin Stowell, *The Historical Performance of Music: An Introduction.* Cambridge Handbooks to the Historical Performance of Music (Cambridge University Press, 1999), chapter 1.
3. Otto Langey, *Practical Tutor for the French Horn* (London: Hawkes, 1910), p. 23.
4. Record number: Disque Gramophone L-753.
5. Record number: Victor 17174.
6. Morley-Pegge/Blandford Correspondence (Bate Collection, Oxford University Music Faculty).
7. Reginald Morley-Pegge, *The French Horn* (London: Benn, 1960; 2nd edn, 1973).
8. Birchard Coar, *Critical Study of the 19th Century Virtuosi in France* (De Kalb, Illinois: Coar, 1952).
9. Birchard Coar, *The French Horn* (De Kalb, Illinois: Coar, 1947, reprinted 1971).
10. Hans Pizka, *Dictionary for Hornists* (Munich: Pizka, 1986).
11. Horace Fitzpatrick, *The Horn and Horn Playing and the Austro Bohemian Tradition, 1680–1830* (Oxford University Press, 1970).
12. Bernhard Brüchle and Kurt Janetzky, *A Pictorial History of the Horn* (Tutzing: Hans Schneider, 1976).
13. Bernhard Brüchle and Kurt Janetzky, *The Horn* (London: Batsford, 1988).
14. Robin Gregory, *The Horn: A Comprehensive Guide to the Modern Instrument and its Music* (London: Faber, 1961; 2nd edn, revised, 1969).
15. Barry Tuckwell, *Horn,* Yehudi Menuhin Music Guides (London: Macdonald, 1983).
16. Jeremy Montagu, *The French Horn* (Princes Risborough: Shire Publications, 1990).
17. Anthony Baines, *Brass Instruments: Their History and Development* (London: Faber, 1976).

18. *Cambridge Companion to Brass Instruments*, ed. Trevor Herbert and John Wallace (Cambridge University Press, 1997).
19. Morley-Pegge/Blandford Correspondence, letter from Blandford, 5 September 1930.
20. Louis-François Dauprat, *Méthode de Cor Alto et Cor Basse* (Paris: Zetter, 1824); translated by Viola Roth (Bloomington, Indiana: Birdalone Music, 1994).
21. Pierre-Joseph Meifred, *Méthode pour le Cor Chromatique ou à pistons* (Paris: Richault, 1841 and Paris: Richault, 1868).
22. Charles Tully, *Tutor for the French Horn* (London: R.Cocks, 1840).

2 Historical background

1. Michael Tippett, *Those Twentieth Century Blues* (London: Hutchinson, 1991), p. 210.
2. Quoted in Morley-Pegge, *The French Horn*, p. 80.
3. *Ibid.*, p. 16.
4. Milan Poštolka, *Count Franz Anton Sporck*, New Grove Dictionary of Music and Musicians, ed. Stanley Sadie, 20 vols. (London: Macmillan, 1980), vol. 18, p. 26.
5. Thomas Hiebert, 'The Horn in the Baroque and Classical Periods', *Cambridge Companion to Brass Instruments* (Cambridge University Press, 1997), p. 104.
6. *Ibid.*, p. 105.
7. Morley-Pegge, *The French Horn*, p. 140.
8. Thomas Hiebert, 'Virtuosity, Experimentation and Innovation in Horn Writing from Early 18th Century Dresden', *Historic Brass Society Journal*, 4 (1992), 116.
9. Manuscript Kat. Wenster Litt. 1/1–17b, Universitetsbiblioteket Lund. *See also* Mary Rasmussen, 'A Contribution to the History of the Baroque Horn Concerto', *Brass Quarterly*, 5 no. 4 (Summer 1962), 135–52.
19. Hiebert, 'Virtuosity', p. 122.
11. Rasmussen, 'A Contribution', p. 146.
12. Hiebert, 'Virtuosity', p. 122.
13. Joseph Fröhlich, 'Horn', in J.S. Ersch and J.G.Grüber, *Allgemeine Encyclopädie der Wissenschaften und Künste*; 3 Sections (Leipzig: F.A Brockhaus, 1818–89); 2/11, *H-N*, ed. G. Hassel and W. Müller, (1834), p. 7.
14. Heinrich Domnich, *Méthode de Premier et de Second Cor* (Paris Conservatoire, 1807), preface, p. iv; translated in Morley-Pegge, *The French Horn*, p. 88.
15. Morley-Pegge, *The French Horn*, p. 202.
16. Karl Haudek, 28 *Duets*, ed. Christopher Larkin, The Rare Brass Series, London Gabrieli Brass Edition, 1994.

17. *Mercure de France*, May 1770 p. 164; quoted in Fitzpatrick, *The Horn*, p. 164.

18. Joseph Fröhlich, writing in Ersch and Grüber, *Allgemeine Encyclopädie*, 2/11, p. 7.

19. *New Instructions for the French Horn*, London: Longman and Broderip, c. 1780, p. 4.

20. Charles Burney, in Abraham Rees, *Cyclopaedia, or Universal Dictionary of Arts, Sciences and Literature*, 39 vols. (London: Longman, Hurst, Rees, Orme & Brown, 1819), vol. 18 (not paginated).

21. John Hawkins, *A General History of the Science and Practice of Music*, London: T. Payne, 1776; 3 vols. (London: Novello, Ewer & Co., 1875), vol. 2, p. 612.

22. H.C. Robbins Landon, *Haydn at Eszterháza, 1766–1790*, (Haydn: Chronicles and Works, 5 vols.), vol. 2, (London: Thames and Hudson, 1976).

23. Sterling E. Murray, 3. *Oettingen*, New Grove Dictionary of Music and Musicians, ed. Stanley Sadie, 20 vols. (London: Macmillan, 1980), vol. 13, pp. 507–8.

24. *Forrest Harmony. Book the Second: Being a Collection of the most Celebrated Aires, made on purpose for two French Horns by the greatest Masters* (London: John Walsh, 1733).

25. Author's collection.

26. Mr Charles, 'Twelve Duettos for two French Horns or two German Flutes'; published in *Apollo's Cabinet or The Muses' Delight* (Liverpool: John Sadler, 1757).

27. *A Collection of duets for French horns to which is added some trios or club pieces for three horns. Composed by Mr Humple, Mr Rathgen, Mr Seibst and Mr Dauche* (London: Jonathan Fentum, c. 1764).

28. Valentine Holmes, *Twenty four Duetts in a pleasing taste for Two French-Horns or two Guittars as also for Two German-Flutes or two Violins* (London: Jonathan Fentum, 1764).

29. William Bates, *Eighteen Duettinos for Two Guittars, Two French Horns or Two Clarinetts* (London: Longman, c. 1767–9).

30. Horace Fitzpatrick, *Türrschmidt*, New Grove Dictionary of Music and Musicians, ed. Stanley Sadie, 20 vols. (London: Macmillan, 1980), vol. 19, p. 284.

31. A case study of Mozart's Serenade for 13 Instruments, K361, is included in: Colin Lawson and Robin Stowell, *The Historical Performance of Music: An Introduction*, Cambridge Handbooks to the Historical Performance of Music (Cambridge University Press, 1999), pp. 109–24.

32. Franz Krommer, attrib., *Partita in E♭*, Northridge, California: Wind Instrument New Dawn Society; information on its authenticity from Karel Padrta, *Franz Krommer* (Prague: Supraphon, 1997), p. 133, and Marshall Stoneham, Jon A.

Gillaspie and David Lindsay Clark, *Wind Ensemble Source Book and Biographical Guide* (Westport, Conn.: Greenwood Press, 1997).

33. Friedrich Schneider, writing in *Allgemeine Musikalische Zeitung* (Leipzig, 26 November 1817), col. 816.

34. Morley-Pegge/Blandford Correspondence, letter from Morley-Pegge, 23 August 1921

35. Millard Myron Laing, *Anton Reicha's Quintets for Flute, Oboe Clarinet, Horn and Bassoon*, Doctoral Dissertation, University of Michigan, 1952: publ. in 2 vols. (Ann Arbor, Michigan: UMI Dissertation Services, 1994), vol. 1, p. 66.

36. Dauprat, *Méthode*, p. 13.

37. Meifred, *Méthode*, p. 4 (Costallat edition).

38. Jean Mohr, *Méthode de premier et de second cor* (Paris: Léon Escudier, 1871).

39. Rudolph Bay, *Af Rud. Bays Efterladte Papirer*, 3 vols. (*Memoirer og Breve*, vols. 43–4, Copenhagen: 1920),vol. 1, p. 137; entry for 17 September 1816; translated, in a letter, by Kjell Moseng.

40. Heinrich Domnich, *Méthode de Premier et de Second Cor* (Paris Conservatoire, 1807), preface p. vii; translated in Coar, *Critical Study*, p. 27.

41. F.J. Fétis, writing in *Revue et Gazette Musicale*, 1865, pp. 215–16; quoted in Coar, *Virtuosi*, p. 131.

42. Morley-Pegge, *The French Horn*, p. 4.

43. Morley-Pegge/Blandford Correspondence, letter from Blandford, 23 August 1921.

44. J.R. Lewy, *Douze Etudes pour le Cor chromatique et le Cor simple* (Leipzig: Breitkopf and Härtel, 1850); quoted in Morley Pegge, *Horn*, p. 211.

45. Franz Ludwig Schubert, 'Über den Gebrauch und Missbrauch der Ventilinstrumente in Verbindung mit andere Instrumenten', *Neue Zeitschrift für Musik*, vol. 61, (Leipzig: Kahnt, 18th August 1865), p. 296.

46. Friedrich Gumbert, *Praktische Horn-Schule* (Leipzig: Forberg, 1879), p. 3. There is confusion over the spelling of Gumbert's name, which is sometimes given as Gumpert. According to Barry Tuckwell (in Tuckwell, *Horn*, p. 137), he was born as Gumpert, but changed his name so that it was the same as that of a popular singer of the day.

47. Richard Wagner, *Tristan und Isolde*, Leipzig, 1860 (preface to the full score).

48. Adam Wirth, *Praktische, systematisch geordnete Hornschule, op 43* (Offenbach: André, 1877), p. 21.

49. Carl Klotz, *Praktische Schule für das einfache u. Chromatische Horn* (Offenbach: André, 1863), p. 4.

50. Algernon Rose, *Talks with Bandsmen* (London, William Rider, 1895; reprinted London: Tony Bingham, no date, *c.* 1996), p. 88.

51. *Grand Method for the French Horn, by Meifred, Gallay and Dauprat* (London: Lafleur, 1880), p. 1.

52. Morley-Pegge/Blandford Correspondence; Blandford 25 September 1945.

53. Concert programme, British Library.

54. Information from Royal Society of Musicians' Archives.

55. *The Harmonicon* (London: Samuel Leigh, 1830), p. 320.

56. Information from Royal Society of Musicians' Archives.

57. *Illustrated London News*, 20 April 1850.

58. Information from Royal Academy of Music's Archives.

59. W.W. Cazalet, *The History of the Royal Academy of Music* (London: Bosworth, 1854), p. 294.

60. See also, John Humphries, 'The Royal Academy of Music and its Traditions', *Brass Bulletin 101* (1998), 42–52.

61. Karl Nödl, *Posthumous Papers*; quoted in Brüchle and Janetzky, *A Pictorial History*, p. 253.

62. Pizka, *Dictionary*, p. 187.

63. Bay, *Af Rud. Bays Efterlade Papirer*, vol. 3, *Musicalsk Rejse*, 1842–3, p. 41.

64. Renato Meucci, transl. Enrico Pelliti, 'The Pelliti Firm: Makers of Brass Instruments in 19th Century Milan', *Historical Brass Society Journal*, 6 (1994), 328, note 32.

65. A.Tosoroni, *Metodo per Corno a 3 pistoni* (Milan: Lucca, after 1840), Tosoroni's Method is referred to in Bernhard Brüchle and Daniel Lienhard, *Horn Bibliographie*, Wilhelmshaven: Heinrichschofen, 1983), vol. 3, p. 23.

66. Raniero Cacciamani, *Metodo d'Istruzione par Corno da Caccia* (Milan: Ricordi, c. 1860).

67. Meucci, 'The Pelliti Firm', p. 329, note 32.

3 Equipment

1. For a fuller discussion of the earliest surviving instruments, see Morley-Pegge, *The French Horn*, chapter 2, and Fitzpatrick, *The Horn*, chapter 3.

2. Reginald Morley-Pegge, revised Frank Hawkins and Richard Merewether, *Horn*, New Grove Dictionary of Music and Musicians, ed. Stanley Sadie, 20 vols. (London: Macmillan, 1980) vol. 8, p. 706.

3. Tully, *Tutor*, p. 1.

4. Morley-Pegge, *Horn* (New Grove), p. 707.

5. *Ibid.*

6. Herbert Heyde, *Das Ventilblasinstrument* (Wiesbaden: Breitkopf und Härtel, 1987), p. 14.

7. Morley-Pegge, *The French Horn*, pp. 26–30.

8. *Divertimento for horn, two violins and basso performed . . . upon Clagget's Patent French Horn*; copies in Bodleian Library, Oxford (shelfmark: Mus. Instr. I, 235(45) and British Library (shelfmark h.127(23)).

9. Friedrich Schneider, writing in *Allgemeine Musikalische Zeitung*, June 1819, col. 416.

10. Morley-Pegge, *The French Horn*, p. 32.

11. Patented 12 July 1830. See, Reine Dahlqvist, 'Some Notes on the Early Valve', *Galpin Society Journal* 33 (1980), 111.

12. Andreas Nemetz, *Hornschule für das einfache Maschin und Signalhorn, op. 18* (Vienna: Diabelli, 1829), quoted, including picture, in Dahlqvist, *Some Notes*, p. 113.

13. Dahlqvist, 'Some Notes', p. 118.

14. Philip Bate, *Valve*, New Grove Dictionary of Music and Musicians, ed. Stanley Sadie, 20 vols. (London: Macmillan, 1980), vol.19, p. 515.

15. For an extensive description of Chaussier's instrument, see Morley-Pegge, *The French Horn*, pp. 63–6.

16. Morley-Pegge/Blandford Correspondence; Morley-Pegge, 22 August 1922.

17. Dauprat, *Méthode*, p. 371.

18. Morley-Pegge, *The French Horn*, p. 115.

19. *Deutscher Musiker-Zeitung, 20th August 1898* (Berlin); quoted extensively in Pizka, *Dictionary*, pp. 279–91.

20. Pizka, *Dictionary*, p. 289.

21. *Ibid.*, p. 480.

22. Eva-Maria Duttenhöfer, *Gebrüder Alexander: 200 Jahre Musikinstrumentenbau in Mainz* (Mainz: Schott, 1982), p. 66.

23. Gounod, *Méthode*, p. 10.

24. Jeffrey Snedeker, 'Joseph Meifred's Méthode pour le cor chromatique ou à pistons', *Historical Brass Society Journal*, 4 (1992), 98.

25. Author's collection.

26. Morley-Pegge, *The French Horn*, p. 110.

27. Lucien Thévet, *Méthode Complète de Cor*, 2 vols. (Paris, Leduc, 1960), vol. 1, p. 6.

28. Morley-Pegge, *The French Horn*, p. 166.

29. Meucci, 'The Pelliti Firm', p. 308.

30. Morley-Pegge, *The French Horn*, p. 39.

31. Pizka, *Dictionary*, p. 523.

32. *The Harmonicon*, 1830, p. 370.

33. Ebenezer Prout, *The Orchestra*, 2 vols. (London, Augener, 1897), vol. 1, p. 192.

34. Author's collection.

35. Copied at the Royal Academy of Music, and reproduced in Humphries, 'The Royal Academy of Music', p. 49. This is probably the 1821 Raoux horn which Puzzi owned, and on which, with the addition of a set of valves, Borsdorf played for most of his career.

36. Morley-Pegge/Blandford Correspondence; Blandford, 24 November 1922.

37. Copy in author's collection.

38. *Grand Method (Meifred, Gallay and Dauprat)*.

39. E.H. Turpin, *Some Observations on the Manipulations of Modern Wind Instruments* (London: Weekes and Co., 1883), pp. 23–4.

40. William H. Stone, *Horn, A Dictionary of Music and Musicians*, ed. Sir George Grove, 4 vols. (London: Macmillan, 1900), vol. 1, p. 747.

41. William H. Stone, rev. D.J. Blaikley, *Horn, Grove's Dictionary of Music and Musicians*, ed. J.A. Fuller-Maitland, 5 vols., (London: Macmillan, 1910), vol. 2, p. 431.

42. Enrico Weller, 'Zur Geschichte des Musikinstrumentenbaus im Vogtland und in Westböhmen', *Rohrblatt*, 11 (1996), 3/4.

43. Heyde, *Das Ventilblasinstrument*, p. 74.

44. A detailed account of influences on the work of the Czech border manufacturers in the late eighteenth century can be found in Karl F. Hachenberg, translated Howard Weiner, 'The complaint of the Markneukirchen brass-instrument [*sic*] makers about the poor quality of brass from the Rodewisch Foundry 1787–1795', *Historic Brass Society Journal*, 10 (1998), 116–45.

45. George Bernard Shaw, *Music in London, 1890–1984*, 3 vols. (London: Constable, 1932), vol. 2, p. 113. Quoted by permission of The Society of Authors, on behalf of the Bernard Shaw Estate

46. Clifford Bevan, *The Tuba Family* (London: Faber & Faber, 1978), p. 195.

47. Baines, *Brass Instruments*, p. 264.

48. Duttenhöfer, *Gebrüder Alexander*, p. 62.

49. Bevan, *The Tuba Family*, p. 196.

50. *New Instructions* (*c.* 1780), p. 2.

51. Joseph Fröhlich, *Vollständige Theoretisch–praktische Musikschule für all beym Orchester gebräuchliche wichtigere Instrumente zum Gebrauch für Musikdirectoren-Lehrer und Liebhaber*, 4 parts (Bonn: Simrock, 1811), Part 3, *Vom Horn*, p. 7.

52. Morley-Pegge/Blandford Correspondence; Blandford 23 November 1924.

53. Morley-Pegge/Blandford Correspondence; Blandford 26 July 1937.

54. Morley-Pegge/Blandford Correspondence; Blandford 26 July 1942.

55. Morley-Pegge, *The French Horn*, p. 102.

56. Dauprat, *Méthode*, p. 20.

57. Fröhlich, Joseph, *Horn*, in J.S.Ersch and J.G. Grüber, *Encyclopädie*, 2/11, p. 7.

58. Wirth, *Praktische, systematisch geordnete Hornschule*; drawing of mute opposite p. 7.

59. A.Lagard, *Méthode de cor d'harmonie* (Paris, Ikelmer Frères, 1878), p. 7.

60. Langey, *Practical Tutor*, p. 23.

61. Personal communication from Trevor Herbert.

62. Personal communication from Anthony Halstead.

63. Langey, *Practical Tutor*, back cover.

64. Morley-Pegge/Blandford Correspondence; Morley-Pegge 18 October 1927.

4 Technique

1. Christopher Winch, attrib., *The Compleat Tutor for the French Horn containing the best and easiest instructions for learners to obtain a proficiency after a perfect new method by Mr Winch and other eminent Masters*, (London: John Simpson, 1746, and London: Peter Thompson, 1756).

2. Source of Winch's first name is Betty Matthews, *Members of the Royal Society of Musicians, 1738–1984* (London: Royal Society of Musicians, 1985), p. 15.

3. Quoted in Morley-Pegge, *The French Horn*, p. 86.

4. Christopher Winch, attrib., *The French Horn Master. Being the best Instructions ever published for the attaining to Perfection on that Instrument* (London: H.Waylett, *c.* 1750).

5. *Apollo's Cabinet or the Muses' Delight. Instructions for the French Horn* (Liverpool: John Sadler, 1757).

6. New Instructions (*c.* 1780), p. 1.

7. Othon Vandenbroek, *Méthode nouvelle et raisonée pour apprendre à donner du Cor* (Paris: 1797); quoted in Morley-Pegge, *The French Horn*, pp. 94–5.

8. Frédéric Duvernoy, *Méthode pour le Cor* (Paris: A l'Imprimerie du Conservatoire de Musique, 1803, and Bonn: Simrock, 1830).

9. George Kastner, *Méthode élémentaire pour le Cor* (Paris: E.Troupenas, 1840).

10. Charles Gounod, *Méthode de Cor à pistons* (Paris: Colombier, *c.* 1845).

11. Haumuller, *Méthode élémentaire de Cor à pistons* (Paris: Schonenberger, 1845).

12. Donatien Urbin, *Méthode de Cor à trois pistons ou cylindres* (Paris: Richault, 1852).

13. François Jacqmin, *Méthode complète de premier et second Cor* (Paris: A.Petit, 1832).

14. Jean-Baptiste Mengal, *Méthode de Cor et Cor à pistons* (Paris: Meissonnier, 1835).

15. Jacques-François Gallay, *Méthode Pour le Cor, op. 54*, (Paris: Colombier, *c.* 1845).

16. J. Blanc, *Grande Méthode de Cor, suivie d'un traité complète de Cor à pistons* (Paris: Grus ainé, *c.* 1855)

17. Mohr, *Méthode*.

18. Lagard, *Méthode*.

19. Fröhlich, *Vollständige Theoretisch-pracktische Musikschule: Vom Horn*.

20. J.H. Göroldt, *Ausführliche theoretisch-praktische Hornschule vom ersten Elementar-Unterricht, bis zur vollkommensten Ausbildung* (Quedlinburg: Basse, 1822).

21. Nemetz, *Hornschule*.

22. *New Instructions* (*c.* 1780), p. 3.

23. Dauprat, *Méthode*, p. 362.

24. *Ibid.*, p. 22.

25. Fröhlich, *Vollständige Theoretisch-pracktische Musikschule: Vom Horn*, p. 6.

26. Tully, *Tutor*, p. 4.

27. Morley-Pegge/Blandford Correspondence; Blandford 20 June 1939 and Morley-Pegge 22 October 1924.

28. Edward Tarr, transl. S.E. Plank and Edward Tarr, *The Trumpet* (London: Batsford, 1988), p. 122.

29. Personal communication from Barry Tuckwell.

30. Richard Merewether, *The Horn, the Horn* (London: Paxman, 1978), p. 33–53.

31. Dauprat, *Méthode*, pp. 22–3.

32. Gallay, *Méthode*, p. 4.

33. Duvernoy, *Méthode*, p. 13 (Simrock edition).

34. Fröhlich, *Vollständige Theoretisch-pracktische Musikschule: Vom Horn*, p. 16.

35. Domnich, *Méthode*, preface p. vii.

36. Dauprat, *Méthode*, p. 34.

37. *Ibid.*, p. 37.

38. Fröhlich, *Vollständige Theoretisch-pracktische Musikschule: Vom Horn*, p. 15.

39. Domnich, *Méthode*, p. 10.

40. Dauprat, *Méthode*, p. 206.

41. Meifred, *Méthode*, p. 32 (Costallat edition).

42. Schubert, Über den Gebrauch und Missbrauch der Ventilinstrumenten', in *Neue Zeitschrift für Musik*, 61 (18 August 1865), 296.

43. Morley-Pegge/Blandford Correspondence; Blandford 18 December 1938.

44. Richard Wagner, *Tristan und Isolde* (Leipzig, 1860), preface to the full score.
45. Mengal, *Méthode*, p. 3.
46. Winch, attrib., *The Compleat Tutor*, p. 2.
47. Domnich, *Méthode*, p. 29.
48. Winch, attrib., *The Compleat Tutor*, p. 1.
49. Tully, *Tutor*, p. 4.
50. Oscar Franz, *Grosse theoretisch-praktische Waldhorn-Schule* (Dresden: J.G. Seeling, *c.* 1880); translated as *School for the Horn*, ed. Thomas Busby (London: Hawkes, 1902), pp. 11 and 12.
51. Fitzpatrick, *The Horn*, p. 109.
52. Tuckwell, *Horn*, p. 162.
53. Dauprat, *Méthode*, p. 23.
54. *New Instructions* (*c.* 1780), p. 4.
55. Baines, *Brass Instruments*, p. 33.
56. Dauprat, *Méthode*, p. 24.
57. Adolphe Sax, *Méthode complète pour saxhorn et saxotromba, soprano, alto, tenor, baryton, basse et contrabasse à 3,4, et 5 cylindres, suivie d'exercices pour l'emploi du compensateur* (Paris: Brandus, 1850).
58. Fröhlich, *Vollständige Theoretisch-pracktische Musikschule: Vom Horn*, p. 8.
59. Lagard, *Méthode*, p. 8.
60. Dauprat, *Méthode*, p. 25.
61. Johann Joachim Quantz, *On Playing the Flute*, translated by Edward R. Reilly (London: Faber & Faber, 1966 and 1985), p. 88.
62. Giovanni Punto, *Etude ou Exercice Journalier Ouvrage Périodique pour le Cor* (Offenbach: André, 1801), pp. 4–10.
63. Dauprat, *Méthode*, p. 27.
64. Domnich, *Méthode*, p. 31.
65. Gallay, *Méthode*, p. 7.
66. Dauprat, *Méthode*, p. 420.
67. *Ibid.*, p. 51.
68. *Ibid.* p. 71.
69. Mengal, *Méthode*, p. 18.
70. Domnich, *Méthode*, p. 31.
71. Fröhlich, *Vollständige Theoretisch-pracktische Musikschule: Vom Horn*, p. 17.
72. Klotz, *Praktische Schule*, p. 25.
73. Gallay, *Méthode*, p. 34
74. Horace Fitzpatrick, *Gallay*, New Grove Dictionary of Music and Musicians, ed. Stanley Sadie, 20 vols. (London: Macmillan, 1980), vol. 7, p. 101.

75. Philip Farkas, *The Art of French Horn Playing* (Evanston, Illinois: Summy-Birchard, 1956), p. 77.
76. John Ridgeon, *How Brass Players do it* (Oakham: Brasswind, 1976), p. 4.

5 The language of musical style

1. Dauprat, *Méthode*, p. 353.
2. Bernhard Crusell, *Bernhard Crusell, Tonsättare Klarinetvirtuos: hans dagböcker. Studier i hans konst* (Stockholm, 1977); p. 38; translated, in a letter, by Kjell Moseng.
3. Bay, *Af Rud. Bays Efterladte Papirer*, vol. 1, p. 138; entry for 17 September 1816.
4. N.C.L. Abrahams, *Meddelelser af mit liv* (Copenhagen: 1876); p. 430; translated, in a letter, by Kjell Moseng.
5. Bay, *Af Rud. Bays Efterladte Papirer*, vol. 1, p. 137–8; entry for 17 September 1816.
6. Arnold Dolmetsch, *The Interpretation of Music of the 17th and 18th Centuries* (London: Novello, 1915; revised 1969).
7. Robert Donington, *The Interpretation of Early Music* (London: Faber & Faber, 1963; revised 1974).
8. Thurston Dart, *The Interpretation of Music* (London: Hutchinson, 1954, revised 1967).
9. *Performance Practice: Music after 1600*, ed. Howard Mayer Brown and Stanley Sadie, New Grove Handbooks in Music (London: Macmillan, 1989).
10. Charles Rosen, *The Classical Style* (London: Faber & Faber, 1971).
11. F. Neumann, *Ornamentation in Baroque and Post-Baroque music, with special emphasis on J.S. Bach* (Princeton University Press, 1978).
12. F. Neumann, *Ornamentation in Mozart* (Princeton University Press, 1986).
13. Lawson and Stowell, *The Historical Performance of Music*.
14. Quantz, *On Playing the Flute*.
15. Carl Philipp Emanuel Bach, *Essay on the True Art of Playing Keyboard Instruments* (Berlin, 1753; translated by W.J. Mitchell, NewYork: Cassell, 1949 and London: Eulenburg, 1974).
16. Leopold Mozart, *Complete Violin School* (Augsburg, 1756), translated by Editha Knocker (Oxford University Press, 1948).
17. Daniel Gottlob Türk, transl. Raymond H. Haggh, *School of Clavier Playing* (Lincoln and London: University of Nebraska Press, 1982).
18. Dauprat, *Méthode*.
19. Domnich, *Méthode*.
20. Gallay, *Méthode*.

21. Meifred, *Méthode.*
22. C.P.E. Bach, *Essay,* p. 150.
23. Dauprat, *Méthode,* p. 354.
24. *Ibid.,* p. 44.
25. Türk, *School of Clavier Playing,* p. 103.
26. Dauprat, *Méthode,* p. 18.
27. *Ibid.,* p. 324, note 2.
28. *Ibid.,* p. 53.
29. Leopold Mozart, *Complete Violin School,* p. 203.
30. Quantz, *On Playing the Flute,* p. 165–6.
31. Leopold Mozart, *Complete Violin School,* p. 205.
32. *Jahrbuch der Tonkunst von Wien und Prag,* ed. J.F. von Schönfeld (Prague: 1796), p. 193; quoted in Fitzpatrick, *The Horn,* p. 180.
33. Louis Spohr, *Violin-Schule* (Vienna: Haslinger, 1832), translated by John Bishop (London: Cocks & Co., n.d.), p. 163.
34. Letter from Bradley Strauchen.
35. Peter Muck, *Einhundert Jahre Berliner Philharmonisches Orchester* (Tutzing: Hans Schneider, 1982), vol. 3, p. 105.
36. Morley-Pegge/Blandford Correspondence; Morley-Pegge 11 August 1946.
37. Fröhlich, *Vollständige Theoretisch-pracktische Musikschule: Vom Horn,* p. 20.
38. From *Prager Neue Zeitung,* vol. 39, 1801, p. 473; quoted in Morley-Pegge/Blandford Correspondence; Morley-Pegge 23 August 1921, and in Fitzpatrick, *The Horn,* p. 171.
39. Meifred, *Méthode,* pp. 91–126 (Costallat edition).
40. Quantz, *On Playing the Flute,* p. 180.
41. Türk, *School of Clavier Playing,* p. 300.
42. *Ibid.,* pp. 298–9
43. *Ibid.,* p. 299.
44. *Ibid.,* p. 300.
45. Eva Badura-Skoda, *Cadenza,* New Grove Dictionary of Music and Musicians, ed. Stanley Sadie, 20 vols. (London: Macmillan, 1980), vol. 3, p. 591.
46. Quantz, *On Playing the Flute,* p. 185.
47. Dauprat, *Méthode,* p. 329.
48. Meifred, *Méthode,* pp. 77–80 (Costallat edition).
49. Quantz, *On Playing the Flute,* p. 182.
50. Dauprat, *Méthode,* p. 329.
51. Türk, *School of Clavier Playing,* p. 301.
52. Quantz, *On Playing the Flute,* pp. 99–100.
53. C.P.E. Bach, *Essay,* p. 81.

54. Quantz, *On Playing the Flute*, p. 99.
55. Dauprat, *Méthode*, pp. 148–9.
56. Johann Nepomuk Hummel, *Ausführlich theoretisch-practische Anweisung zum Piano-forte Spiel* (Vienna: Haslinger, 1828); quoted in Robert Donington, *Ornaments*, p. 386.
57. Leopold Mozart, *Complete Violin School*, pp. 190–1.
58. C.P.E. Bach, *Essay*, p. 108.
59. Leopold Mozart, *Complete Violin School*, p. 189.
60. Dauprat, *Méthode*, p. 51.
61. Quantz, *On Playing the Flute*, p. 102.
62. *Ibid.*, p. 103.
63. C.P.E. Bach, *Essay*, p. 103.
64. Quantz, *On Playing the Flute*, p. 91.
65. Dauprat, *Méthode*, p. 150.
66. Quantz, *On Playing the Flute*, p. 99.
67. *Ibid.*, p. 95.
68. Dauprat, *Méthode*, p. 150.
69. *Ibid.*, p. 223.
70. *Ibid.*, p. 78.
71. C.P.E. Bach, *Essay*, p. 157.
72. Quantz, *On Playing the Flute*, p. 67.
73. C.P.E. Bach, *Essay*, p. 149.
74. Leopold Mozart, *Complete Violin School*, p. 139.
75. David Fuller, *Notes Inégales,* New Grove Dictionary of Music and Musicians, ed. Stanley Sadie, 20 vols. (London: Macmillan, 1980), vol.13, p. 420.

6 Case studies

1. 'For you alone are the holy one, you alone are the Lord, you alone are the most high, Jesus Christ.'
2. Philipp Spitta, transl. Clara Bell and J.A. Fuller Maitland, *Johann Sebastian Bach*, 3 vols. (New York: Dover Publications,1951), vol. 3, p. 38.
3. Hiebert, 'Virtuosity', p. 122.
4. Percy Scholes, *The Mirror of Music, 1844–1944*, 2 vols. (London: Novello and Oxford University Press, 1947), vol.1, p. 71, quoting 'The Musical World'.
5. Hiebert, 'Virtuosity', p. 116.
6. Shelfmark, A146.
7. The only known source, a set of parts in the Oettingen–Wallerstein collection at Harburg, was originally headed simply, 'Concerto per due Corni Principale'.

8. *The Breitkopf Thematic Catalogue: the Six Parts and 16 Supplements, 1762–1787* (New York: Dover, 1966), p. 732: Supplement XIV (1781).

9. Shelfmark, Mus. 3356-0-503 Nr. 33.

10. *Documents from the Esterházy Archives in Eisenstadt and Forchtenstein*, edited from *János Hárich's papers*, Haydn Yearbook XVIII, ed. H.C. Robbins Landon (London: Thames & Hudson, 1993), pp. 24–6.

11. Geminiani, Francesco, *A Treatise of Good Taste in the Art of Musick* (London, 1749), p. 4.

12. Domnich, *Méthode*, p. 10.

13. Available in Breitkopf & Härtel's piano reduction.

14. Kat. Wenster Litt. 17a, Universitetsbiblioteket Lund. See chapter 2.

15. Fitzpatrick, *The Horn*, p. 87.

16. In 1990 I was invited to see a private collection which included manuscript copies of some horn duets by 'Sigr. Haudex, Cammer Musicus'. There is good stylistic evidence that they were indeed composed by Karl Haudek (1721 – after 1800), and I was later able to establish that the copies were written on paper which was made at Koenigstein, near Dresden, at the papermill owned by Johann Gottfried Reinhardt, around 1806. The copies' history in this country is well documented, and from this it seems likely that they were brought to England by Adolf Borsdorf, who could have acquired them while studying in Dresden between 1869 and 1874.

17. Jack Westrup, with Neal Zaslaw, *Orchestra, New Grove Dictionary of Music and Musicians*, ed. Stanley Sadie, 20 vols. (London: Macmillan, 1980), vol. 13, p. 690: table by Eleanor Selfridge-Field and Neal Zaslaw.

18. Reproduced in Hans Pizka, *Das Horn bei Mozart* (Kirchheim beim München: Hans Pizka Edition, 1980), pp. 81–92.

19. Shelfmark, Cary 35.

20. Mozart, Wolfgang Amadeus, *Neue Ausgabe sämtlicher Werke*, V/14/5: Hornkonzerte (Kassel: Bärenreiter, 1987).

21. Franz Giegling in Mozart, *Hornkonzerte*; pp. xiii–xiv of preface.

22. In Aloys Fuchs Collection, Prague University Library, shelfmark, MII/16c.

23. Tyson, Alan, *Mozart Studies of the Autograph Scores* (Cambridge, Mass: Harvard University Press, 1987), pp. 246–61: *Mozart's D Major Horn Concerto: Questions of Date and Authenticity*.

24. *Mercure de France*, May 1770; quoted in Fitzpatrick, *The Horn*, p. 164.

25. Alexander Wheelock Thayer, rev. and edited Elliott Forbes, *Thayer's Life of Beethoven*, 2 vols. (Princeton University Press, 1964), vol. 1, p. 166.

26. Franz Wegeler and Ferdinand Ries, translated by Frederick Noonan, *Remembering Beethoven* (London: André Deutsch, 1988), p. 71.

27. Franz Süssmayr, *Sonate pour le Piano-Forte et un Corn de chasse*, manuscript sketches preserved in the British Library (Add. 32181 ff.195–200).

28. *Allgemeine Musikalische Zeitung*, 2 July 1800, col. 704.

29. Thayer, *Life of Beethoven*, vol. 1, pp. 188–9.

30. Morley-Pegge, *The French Horn*, p. 152.

31. *Ibid.*, p. 158.

32. *The Harmonicon*, 1827, p. 56.

33. Otto Eric Deutsch, translated by Eric Blom, *Schubert: A Documentary Biography* (London: J.M. Dent & Sons, 1946), p. 756.

34. *Ibid.*, p. 631.

35. Gottfried Weber, writing in *Caecilia* (Mainz: B.Schott, 1836), p. 265.

36. Hector Berlioz, translated by David Cairns, *The Memoirs of Hector Berlioz* (London: Gollancz, 1969), p. 306.

37. Robert Schumann, translated by May Herbert, *Life of Robert Schumann told in his Letters*, 2 vols. (London: Richard Bentley & Son, 1890); p. 255: Letter to Dr Hermann Härtel, Dresden 2 May 1849.

38. Houghton Library, Harvard University: MS Mus 99.2.

39. Rufus Hallmark, *Auf dem Strom*, Schubert Studies: Problems of style and chronology, ed. E. Badura-Skoda and P. Branscombe (Cambridge University Press, 1982), pp. 25–46.

40. Felix Mendelssohn, translated by Craig Tomlinson, *Felix Mendelssohn: A Life in Letters*, ed. Rudolf Elvers (London: Cassell, 1986); p. 131: letter to Rebecka Mendelssohn-Bartholdy, Vienna 22 August 1830.

41. Berthold Litzmann, *Clara Schumann: ein Künstlerleben*, 3 vols. (Leipzig: Breitkopf & Härtel, 1902), vol.2, p. 183.

42. Chissell, Joan, *Schumann* (London: J.M. Dent & Sons Ltd, 1948, rev. 1967), p. 66.

43. R. Murray Schafer, *ETA Hoffmann and Music* (University of Toronto Press, 1975), pp. 113–14.

44. Brüchle and Janetzky, *A Pictorial History*, p. 228.

45. Berthold Litzmann, *Clara Schumann*, vol. 2, p. 183.

46. Brüchle and Janetzky, *The Horn*, p. 93.

47. Berlioz, *Memoirs*, p. 306.

48. Brüchle and Janetzky, *A Pictorial History*, p. 230.

49. Made without historical precedent but recorded on Elan, CD82260.

50. Johannes Brahms, *Akademische Festouverture*, op. 80 (Bonn: Simrock, July 1881).

51. Margit L. McCorkle, *Johannes Brahms: Thematisch-Bibliographisches Werkverzeichnis* (Munich: G. Henle Verlag, 1984), p. 145.

52. May, Florence, *The Life of Brahms* (London: William Reeves, 1905; reprinted Neptune City, New Jersey: Paganiniana Publications, Inc. , 1981), p. 368.
53. Albert Dietrich and J.V. Widman, translated Dora E. Hecht, *Recollections of Johannes Brahms* (London: Seeley, 1899), p. 48.
54. May, *The Life of Brahms*, pp. 371–2, quoting letter from Brahms to Albert Dietrich.
55. Heyde, *Das Ventilblasinstrument*, p. 110.
56. Joseph Lindner in *Deutsche Musiker-Zeitung*, 1898; quoted in Pizka, *Dictionary*, p. 281.
57. Litzmann, *Clara Schumann*, vol. 3, p. 198.
58. May, *The Life of Brahms*, pp. 384–5.
59. Hans-Hubert Schönzeler, *Hans Richter*, New Grove Dictionary of Music and Musicians, ed. Stanley Sadie, 20 vols. (London: Macmillan, 1980), vol. 15, p. 847.
60. Manuscript in Library of Congress: Whittall Foundation, Washington DC; facsimile in Johannes Brahms, *Johannes Brahms Autographs: Facsimiles of 8 Manuscripts in the Library of Congress*, Introduction by James Webster; Notes about the manuscripts by George S. Bozarth (New York and London: Garland Publishing, Inc. , 1983); facsimile on pp. 183–222.

Bibliography

Abrahams, N.C.L., *Meddelelser af mit liv* (Copenhagen: 1876).

Allgemeine Musikalische Zeitung [AMZ], ed. F. Rochlitz (Leipzig: Breitkopf and Härtel, 1798–1848).

Apollo's Cabinet or the Muses' Delight (Liverpool: John Sadler, 1757)

Bach, Carl Philipp Emanuel, *Essay on the True Art of Playing Keyboard Instruments* (Berlin, 1753); translated by W.J. Mitchell (New York: Cassell, 1949 and London: Eulenburg, 1974).

Badura-Skoda, Eva, *Cadenza*, New Grove Dictionary of Music and Musicians, ed. Stanley Sadie, 20 vols. (London: Macmillan, 1980), vol. 3, pp. 586–93.

Baines, Anthony, *Brass Instruments: Their History and Development* (London: Faber, 1976).

Bate, Philip, *Valve*, New Grove Dictionary of Music and Musicians, ed. Stanley Sadie, 20 vols. (London: Macmillan, 1980), vol. 19, pp. 510–15.

Bates, William, *Eighteen Duettinos for Two Guittars, Two French Horns or Two Clarinetts* (London: Longman, c. 1767–9).

Bay, Rudolph, *Efterladte Papirer*, 3 vols. (*Memoirer og Breve*, vols 32–34) (Copenhagen, 1920).

Berlioz, Hector, *The Memoirs of Hector Berlioz* (London: Gollancz, 1969) (translated by David Cairns).

Bevan, Clifford, *The Tuba Family* (London: Faber & Faber, 1978).

Blanc, J., *Grande Méthode de Cor, suivie d'un traité complète de Cor à pistons* (Paris: Grus ainé, c. 1855).

Brahms, Johannes, *Akademische Festouverture*, op. 80 (Bonn: Simrock, July 1881).

Johannes Brahms Autographs: Facsimiles of 8 Manuscripts in the Library of Congress, Introduction by James Webster; Notes about the manuscripts by George S. Bozarth, York & London: Garland Publishing, Inc., 1983).

The Breitkopf Thematic Catalogue: the Six Parts and 16 Supplements, 1762–1787, (New York: Dover, 1966), p. 732: Supplement XIV (1781).

Brüchle, Bernhard and Janetzky, Kurt, *The Horn* (London: Batsford, 1988).

A Pictorial History of the Horn (Tutzing: Hans Schneider, 1976).

Brüchle, Bernhard and Lienhard, Daniel, *Horn Bibliographie*, 3 vols., vols. 1–2 by Brüchle; vol. 3 by Lienhard (Wilhelmshaven: Heinrichshofen, 1970–83).

Burney, Charles, *Horn*, in Abraham Rees, *Cyclopaedia, or Universal Dictionary of Arts, Sciences and Literature*, 39 vols. (London: Longman, Hurst, Rees, Orme & Brown, 1819).

Cacciamani, Raniero, *Metodo d'Istruzione par Corno da Caccia* (Milan: Ricordi, *c.* 1860).

Cambridge Companion to Brass Instruments, ed. Trevor Herbert and John Wallace (Cambridge University Press, 1997).

Cazalet, W.W., *The History of the Royal Academy of Music* (London: Bosworth, 1854).

Charles, Mr, 'Twelve Duettos for two French Horns or two German Flutes'; published in *Apollo's Cabinet or The Muses' Delight* (Liverpool: John Sadler, 1757).

Chissell, Joan, *Schumann* (London: J.M. Dent & Sons Ltd, 1948, rev. 1967).

Coar, Birchard, *Critical Study of the 19th Century Horn Virtuosi in France* (De Kalb, Illinois: Coar, 1952).

The French Horn (De Kalb, Illinois: Coar, 1947), reprinted 1971.

A Collection of duets for French horns to which is added some trios or club pieces for three horns. Composed by Mr Humple, Mr Rathgen, Mr Seibst and Mr Dauche (London: Jonathan Fentum, *c.* 1764).

Crusell, Bernhard, *Bernhard Crusell, Tonsättare Klarinetvirtuos: hans dagböcker. Studier i hans konst* (Stockholm, 1977).

Dahlqvist, Reine, Some Notes on the Early Valve, *Galpin Society Journal*, 33 (1980), 111–24.

Dart, Thurston, *The Interpretation of Music* (London: Hutchinson, 1954, revised 1967).

Dauprat, Louis-François, *Méthode de Cor Alto et Cor Basse* (Paris: Zetter, 1824); (Bloomington, Indiana: Birdalone Music, 1994), translated by Viola Roth.

Deutsch, Otto Eric, translated by Eric Blom, *Schubert: A Documentary Biography* (London: J.M. Dent & Sons, 1946).

Deutscher Musiker-Zeitung (Berlin).

A Dictionary of Music and Musicians, ed. Sir George Grove, 4 vols. (London: Macmillan, 1900).

Dietrich, Albert and Widman, J.V., translated Dora E. Hecht, *Recollections of Johannes Brahms* (London: Seeley, 1899, p. 48).

Divertimento for horn, two violins and basso performed . . . upon Clagget's Patent French Horn; copies in Bodleian Library, Oxford (shelfmark: Mus.Instr. I, 235 (45) and British Library (shelfmark h.127(23)).

Documents from the Esterházy Archives in Eisenstadt and Forchtenstein, edited from János Hárich's papers, Haydn Yearbook XVIII, ed. H.C. Robbins Landon (London: Thames & Hudson, 1993), pp. 1–110.

Dolmetsch, Arnold, *The Interpretation of Music of the 17th and 18th Centuries* (London: Novello, 1915), revised 1969.

Domnich, Heinrich, *Méthode de Premier et de Second Cor* (Paris Conservatoire, 1807).

Donington, Robert, *The Interpretation of Early Music* (London: Faber & Faber, 1963), revised 1974.

Ornaments, New Grove Dictionary of Music and Musicians, ed. Stanley Sadie, 20 vols. (London: Macmillan, 1980), vol. 13, pp. 827–67.

Duttenhöfer, Eva-Maria, *Gebrüder Alexander: 200 Jahre Musikinstrumentenbau in Mainz* (Mainz: Schott, 1982).

Duvernoy, Frédéric, *Méthode pour le Cor* (Paris: A l'Imprimerie du Conservatoire de Musique, 1803, and Bonn: Simrock, 1830).

Ersch, J.S. and Grüber, J.G. *Allgemeine Encyclopädie der Wissenschaften und Künste* (Leipzig: F.A. Brockhaus, 1818–89).

Farkas, Philip, *The Art of French Horn Playing* (Evanston, Illinois: Summy-Birchard, 1956).

Fétis, F.J., writing in *Revue et Gazette Musicale*, 1865, pp. 215–16; quoted in Coar, *Virtuosi.*

Fitzpatrick, Horace, *The Horn and Horn Playing and the Austro Bohemian Tradition, 1680–1830* (Oxford University Press, 1970).

Gallay, New Grove Dictionary of Music and Musicians, ed. Stanley Sadie, 20 vols. (London: Macmillan, 1980), vol. 7, p. 101.

Türrschmidt, New Grove Dictionary of Music and Musicians, ed. Stanley Sadie, 20 vols. (London: Macmillan, 1980), vol. 19, p. 284.

Forrest Harmony. Book the Second: Being a Collection of the most Celebrated Aires, made on purpose for two French Horns by the greatest Masters (London: John Walsh, 1733).

Franz, Oscar, *Grosse theoretisch-praktische Waldhorn-Schule* (Dresden: J.G. Seeling, c. 1880), translated as *School for the Horn*, ed. Thomas Busby (London: Hawkes, 1902).

Fröhlich, Joseph, 'Horn', in J.S. Ersch and J.G. Grüber, *Allgemeine Encyclopädie der Wissenschaften und Künste* (Leipzig: F.A. Brockhaus, 1818–89).

Vollständige Theoretisch-pracktische Musikschule für all beym Orchester gebräuchliche wichtigere Instrumente zum Gebrauch für Musikdirectoren-Lehrer und Liebhaber (Bonn: Simrock, 1811).

Fuller, David, *Notes Inégales*, New Grove Dictionary of Music and Musicians, ed. Stanley Sadie, 20 vols. (London: Macmillan, 1980), vol. 13, pp. 420–7.

Gallay, Jacques-François, *Méthode Pour le Cor, op. 54* (Paris: Colombier, *c.* 1845).

Geminiani, F., *A Treatise of Good Taste in the Art of Musick* (London, 1749, rev. 1969), p. 4, quoted in Donington, *Ornaments*.

Göroldt, J.H., *Ausführliche theoretisch-praktische Hornschule vom ersten Elementar-Unterricht, bis zur vollkommensten Ausbildung* (Quedlinburg: Basse, 1822).

Gounod, Charles, *Méthode de Cor à pistons* (Paris: Colombier, *c.* 1845).

Grand Method for the French Horn, by Meifred, Gallay and Dauprat (London: Lafleur, 1880).

Gregory, Robin, *The Horn: A Comprehensive Guide to the Modern Instrument and its Music* (London: Faber, 1961; 2nd edn, revised, 1969).

Gumbert, Friedrich, *Praktische Horn-Schule* (Leipzig: Forberg, 1879).

Hachenberg, Karl F., translated Howard Weiner, 'The complaint of the Markneukirchen brass-instrument [*sic*] makers about the poor quality of brass from the Rodewisch Foundry, 1787–1795', *Historic Brass Society Journal*, 10 (1998), 116–45.

Hallmark, Rufus, *Auf dem Strom*, Schubert Studies: Problems of style and chronology, ed. E.Badura-Skoda and P. Branscombe (Cambridge University Press, 1982).

The Harmonicon (London: Samuel Leigh, 1830).

Haudek, Karl, *28 Duets*, ed. Christopher Larkin, The Rare Brass Series (London Gabrieli Brass Edition, 1994).

Haumuller, *Méthode élémentaire de Cor à pistons* (Paris: Schonenberger, 1845).

Hawkins, John, *A General History of the Science and Practice of Music* (London: T. Payne, 1776; London: Novello, Ewer & Co., 1875).

Heyde, Herbert, *Das Ventilblasinstrument* (Wiesbaden: Breitkopf und Härtel, 1987).

Hiebert, Thomas, 'The Horn in the Baroque and Classical Periods', *Cambridge Companion to Brass Instruments* (Cambridge University Press, 1997), pp. 103–14.

'Virtuosity, Experimentation and Innovation in Horn Writing from early 18th Century Dresden', *Historic Brass Society Journal*, 4 (1992), pp. 112–39.

Holmes, Valentine, *Twenty four Duetts in a pleasing taste for Two French-Horns or two Guittars as also for Two German-Flutes or two Violins* (London: Jonathan Fentum, 1764).

Hummel, Johann Nepomuk, *Ausführlich theoretisch-practische Anweisung zum Piano-forte Spiel* (Vienna: Haslinger, 1828), quoted in Robert Donington, *Ornaments*.

Humphries, John, 'The Royal Academy of Music and its Traditions', *Brass Bulletin* 101 (1998), 42–52.

Illustrated London News (London: George C. Leighton).

Jacqmin, François, *Méthode complète de premier et second Cor* (Paris: A. Petit, 1832).

Jahrbuch der Tonkunst von Wien und Prag, ed. J.F. von Schönfeld (Prague: 1796).

Kastner, George, *Méthode élémentaire pour le Cor* (Paris: E.Troupenas, 1840).

Klotz, Carl, *Praktische Schule für das einfache u. Chromatische Horn* (Offenbach: André, 1863).

Krommer, Franz, attrib., *Partita in E flat* (Northridge, California: Wind Instrument New Dawn Society, no date).

Lagard, A, *Méthode de cor d'harmonie* (Paris, Ikelmer Frères, 1878).

Laing, Millard Myron, *Anton Reicha's Quintets for Flute, Oboe, Clarinet, Horn and Bassoon*, Doctoral Dissertation, University of Michigan, 1952: publ. in 2 vols., (Ann Arbor, Michigan: UMI Dissertation Services, 1994).

Langey, Otto, *Practical Tutor for the French Horn* (London: Hawkes, 1910).

Lawson, Colin and Stowell, Robin, *The Historical Performance of Music: An Introduction*, Cambridge Handbooks to the Historical Performance of Music (Cambridge University Press, 1999).

Lewy, J.R., *Douze Etudes pour le Cor chromatique et le Cor simple* (Leipzig: Breitkopf and Härtel, 1850).

Litzmann, Berthold, *Clara Schumann: ein Künstlerleben* (Leipzig: Breitkopf and Härtel, 1902).

McCorkle, Margit L. *Johannes Brahms: Thematisch-Bibliographisches Werkverzeichnis* (Munich: G. Henle Verlag, 1984); Horn Trio, op. 40: pp. 144–7.

Manuscript Kat. Wenster Litt. 1/1-17b, Universitetsbiblioteket Lund.

Matthews, Betty, *Members of the Royal Society of Musicians, 1738–1984* (London: Royal Society of Musicians, 1985).

May, Florence, *The Life of Brahms* (London: William Reeves, 1905); reprinted Neptune City (New Jersey: Paganiniana Publications, Inc., 1981).

Meifred, Pierre-Joseph, *Méthode pour le Cor Chromatique ou à pistons* (Paris: Richault, 1841 and Paris: Richault, 1868, reprinted after 1901 in Paris by Costallat).

Mendelssohn, Felix, translated by Craig Tomlinson, *Felix Mendelssohn: A Life in Letters*, ed. Rudolf Elvers (London: Cassell, 1986).

Mengal, Jean-Baptiste, *Méthode de Cor et Cor à pistons* (Paris: Meissonnier, 1835).

Mercure de France, May 1770, p. 164; quoted in Fitzpatrick, *The Horn*, p. 164.

Merewether, Richard, *The Horn, the Horn* (London: Paxman, 1978).

Meucci, Renato, translated by Enrico Pelliti, 'The Pelliti Firm: Makers of Brass

Instruments in 19th Century Milan', *Historical Brass Society Journal*, 6 (1994), 304–33.

Mohr, Jean, *Méthode de premier et de second cor* (Paris: Léon Escudier, 1871).

Montagu, Jeremy, *The French Horn* (Princes Risborough: Shire Publications, 1990).

Morley-Pegge, Reginald, *The French Horn* (London: Benn, 1960; 2nd edn, 1973).

Horn, New Grove Dictionary of Music and Musicians, ed. Stanley Sadie, 20 vols. (London: Macmillan, 1980), vol. 8, pp. 697–712 (revised Frank Hawkins and Richard Merewether).

Morley-Pegge/Blandford Correspondence, Bate Collection, Oxford University Music Faculty.

Mozart, Leopold, *Complete Violin School* (Augsburg, 1756), translated by Editha Knocker (Oxford University Press, 1948).

Mozart, Wolfgang Amadeus, *Neue Ausgabe sämtlicher Werke*, V/14/5: *Hornkonzerte* (Kassel: Bärenreiter, 1987).

Muck, Peter, *Einhundert Jahre Berliner Philharmonisches Orchester*, vols. 1–3 (Tutzing: Hans Schneider, 1982).

Murray, Sterling E., Oettingen, New Grove Dictionary of Music and Musicians, ed. Stanley Sadie, 20 vols. (London: Macmillan, 1980), vol. 13, pp. 507–8.

The Musical Directory, Annual and Almanack, 58th Annual Issue (London: Rudall, Carte and Co., 1910).

The Musical World: A weekly Record of Musical Science, Literature and Intelligence (London: Novello, 1838–1891)

Nemetz, Andreas, *Hornschule für das einfache Maschin und Signalhorn, op. 18* (Vienna: Diabelli, 1829).

Neumann, F., *Ornamentation in Baroque and Post-Baroque Music, with Special Emphasis on J.S. Bach* (Princeton University Press, 1978).

Ornamentation and Improvisation in Mozart (Princeton University Press, 1986).

New Grove Dictionary of Music and Musicians, ed. Stanley Sadie, 20 vols. (London: Macmillan, 1980).

New Instructions for the French Horn (London: Longman and Broderip, c. 1780).

Nödl, Karl, *Posthumous Papers*; quoted in Brüchle and Janetzky, *A Pictorial History*, p. 253

Padrta, Karel, *Franz Krommer* (Prague: Supraphon, 1997).

Performance Practice: Music after 1600, ed. Howard Mayer Brown and Stanley Sadie, New Grove Handbooks in Music (London: Macmillan, 1989).

Pizka, Hans, *Dictionary for Hornists* (Munich: Pizka, 1986).

Das Horn bei Mozart (Kirchheim beim München: Hans Pizka Edition, 1980).

Poštolka, Milan, *Count Franz Anton Sporck*, New Grove Dictionary of Music and

Musicians, ed. Stanley Sadie, 20 vols. (London: Macmillan, 1980), vol. 18, pp. 25–6.

Prager Neue Zeitung, vol. 39, 1801.

Prout, Ebenezer, *The Orchestra*, 2 vols. (London: Augener, 1897).

Punto, Giovanni, *Etude ou Exercice Journalier Ouvrage Périodique pour le Cor* (Offenbach: André, 1801).

Quantz, Johann Joachim, *On Playing the Flute* (Berlin, 1752), translated by Edward R. Reilly (London: Faber & Faber, 1966 and 1985).

Rasmussen, Mary, 'A Contribution to the History of the Baroque Horn Concerto', *Brass Quarterly*, 5 no. 4 (Summer 1962), 135–52.

Rees, Abraham, *Cyclopaedia, or Universal Dictionary of Arts, Sciences and Literature*, 39 vols. (London: Longman, Hurst, Rees, Orme & Brown, 1819).

Ridgeon, John, *How Brass Players do it* (Oakham: Brasswind, 1976).

Riemann, Hugo, *Catechism of Musical Instruments* (Leipzig 1888; English translation, London: Augener, 1888).

Robbins Landon, H.C., *Haydn at Eszterháza, 1766–1790* (Haydn: Chronicles and Works, 5 vols., vol. 2 (London: Thames and Hudson, 1976).

Rose, Algernon, Talks with Bandsmen (London, William Rider, 1895; reprinted London: Tony Bingham, no date, *c.* 1996).

Rosen, Charles, *The Classical Style* (London: Faber & Faber, 1971).

Sax, Adolphe, *Méthode complète pour saxhorn et saxotromba, soprano, alto, tenor, baryton, basse et contrabasse à 3, 4, et 5 cylindres, suivie d'exercices pour l'emploi du compensateur* (Paris: Brandus, 1850).

Schafer, R. Murray, *ETA Hoffmann and Music* (University of Toronto Press, 1975).

Schönzeler, Hans-Hubert, *Hans Richter*, New Grove Dictionary of Music and Musicians, ed. Stanley Sadie, 20 vols. (London: Macmillan, 1980), vol. 15, pp. 847–8.

Scholes, Percy, *The Mirror of Music, 1844–1944* (London: Novello and Oxford University Press, 1947).

Schubert, Franz Ludwig, 'Über den Gebrauch und Missbrauch der Ventilinstrumente in Verbindung mit andere Instrumenten', *Neue Zeitschrift für Musik* (Leipzig: Kahnt, 18 August, 25 August and 1 September 1865), vol. 61, pp. 296–7. 304–5, 312–13.

Schumann, Robert, translated by May Herbert, *Life of Robert Schumann told in his Letters*, 2 vols. (London: Richard Bentley & Son, 1890).

Shaw, George Bernard, *Music in London, 1890–1894*, 3 vols. (London: Constable, 1932).

Snedeker, Jeffrey, 'Joseph Meifred's Méthode pour le cor chromatique ou à pistons', *Historical Brass Society Journal*, 4 (1992), pp. 304–33.

Spitta, Philipp (Clara Bell and J.A. Fuller Maitland trans.), *Johann Sebastian Bach* (New York: Dover Publications, 1951).

Spohr, Louis, *Violin-Schule* (Vienna: Haslinger, 1832), translated by John Bishop (London: Cocks & Co., n.d.).

Stone, William H., *Horn*, A Dictionary of Music and Musicians, ed. Sir George Grove, 4 vols. (London: Macmillan, 1900), vol. 1, pp. 747–52.

Horn, Grove's Dictionary of Music and Musicians, ed. J.A. Fuller-Maitland, 5 vols. (London: Macmillan, 1910), vol. 2, p. 431 (revised D.J. Blaikley).

Stoneham, Marshall, Gillaspie, Jon A. and Lindsay Clark, David, *Wind Ensemble Source Book and Biographical Guide* (Westport, Conn.: Greenwood Press, 1997).

Süssmayr, Franz, *Sonate pour le Piano-Forte et un Corn de chasse*, manuscript preserved in the British Library (Add. 32181 ff.195–200).

Tarr, Edward, transl. S.E. Plank and Edward Tarr, *The Trumpet* (London: Batsford, 1988).

Thayer, Alexander Wheelock, revised and edited Elliott Forbes, *Thayer's Life of Beethoven*, 2 vols. (Princeton University Press, 1964).

Thévet, Lucien, *Méthode Complète de Cor* (Paris, Leduc, 1960).

Tippett, Michael, *Those Twentieth Century Blues* (London: Hutchinson, 1991).

Tosoroni, A., *Metodo per Corno a 3 pistoni* (Milan: Lucca, after 1840).

Tuckwell, Barry, *Horn*, Yehudi Menuhin Music Guides (London: Macdonald, 1983).

Tully, Charles, *Tutor for the French Horn* (London: R. Cocks, 1840).

Türk, Daniel Gottlob, trans. Raymond H. Haggh, *School of Clavier Playing* (Lincoln and London: University of Nebraska Press, 1982).

Turpin, E.H., *Some Observations on the Manipulations of Modern Wind Instruments* (London: Weekes and Co., 1883).

Tyson, Alan, *Mozart Studies of the Autograph Scores* (Cambridge, Mass: Harvard University Press, 1987), pp. 246–61: *Mozart's D Major Horn Concerto: Questions of Date and Authenticity.*

Urbin, Donatien, *Méthode de Cor à trois pistons ou cylindres* (Paris: Richault, 1852).

Vandenbroek, Othon, *Méthode nouvelle et raisonée pour apprendre à donner du Cor* (Paris: 1797).

Wagner, Richard, *Tristan und Isolde* (Leipzig, 1860), preface to the full score.

Weber, Gottfried, untitled review of horn quartets by B.D. Weber in *Caecilia* (Mainz: B.Schott, 1836), pp. 265–7.

Wegeler, Franz and Ries, Ferdinand, translated by Frederick Noonan, *Remembering Beethoven* (London: André Deutsch, 1988).

Weller, Enrico, 'Zur Geschichte des Musikinstrumentenbaus im Vogtland und in Westböhmen', *Rohrblatt*, 11 (1996), 3/4, part 1, 116–22; part 2, 152–62.

Westrup, Jack, with Zaslaw, Neal, *Orchestra*, New Grove Dictionary of Music and Musicians, ed. Stanley Sadie, 20 vols. (London: Macmillan, 1980), vol. 13, pp. 679–91.

Winch, Christopher, attrib., *The Compleat Tutor for the French Horn containing the best and easiest instructions for learners to obtain a Proficiency after a perfect new method by Mr Winch and other eminent Masters* (London: John Simpson, 1746, and London: Peter Thompson: 1756).

attrib., *The French Horn Master. Being the best Instructions ever published for the attaining to Perfection on that Instrument* (London: H.Waylett, c. 1750).

Wirth, Adam, *Praktische, systematisch geordnete Hornschule, op. 43* (Offenbach: André, 1877).

Index

Abrahams, Nicolai Christian Levin (1798–1870), 69
acciaccaturas, 84
Alexander (horn maker), 31, 35, 41, 48
America's Shrine to Music Museum, 50
Andersen, Johan Carl Friderich (1787–1853), 69
André, Johann Anton (1775–1842), 86, 87
Apollo's Cabinet, 51
appoggiaturas, 75, 76–7
articulation, 12, 44, 76, 77, 84, 87
  see also tonguing
Artôt, Jean Désiré Montagney (1803–1887), 21
ascending third valve, 36–7
L'Association Générale des Ouvriers, *33*, 36
Asta, Lorenzo dall' (*fl.* 1822), 25
Austria, 41, 49
  see also Linz; Salzburg; Vienna

Bach, Carl Philipp Emanuel (1714–1788), 70, 75, 76, 77–8
Bach, Johann Sebastian (1685–1750), 8–9, 79, 100
  Art of Fugue, BWV 1080, 100
  Also hat Gott die Welt geliebt, BWV 68, 9
  Brandenburg Concerto no. 1, BWV 1046, 81
  Christmas Oratorio, BWV 248, 8, 81
  Halt im Gedächtnis Jesum Christ, BWV 67, 9
  Jauchzett Gott in allen Landen, BWV 51, 81
  Mass in B minor: Quoniam, BWV 232, 8, 80–2
  Peasant Cantata, BWV 212, 8

  Wär Gott nicht mit uns diese Zeit, BWV 14, 8
  Was mir behagt, BWV 208, 8
  Wie schön leuchtet der Morgenstern, BWV 1, 8, 81
Badia, Carlo Agostino (1672–1738), 8
Baines, Anthony (1912–1997), 4
Baneux, Mathieu Gustave (1825–1878), 20
Barboteu, Georges (*b.* 1924), 36, 72
Baroque horn, 5, 8–9, 46–7, 51, 52–4, 55, 80,
Bate Collection, Oxford University, 4, 34, 49
Bates, William (*fl. c.* 1750–*c.* 1780), 14
Baumann, Hermann Rudolf Konrad (*b.* 1934), 4
Bay, Rudolph (1791–1856), 25, 69
Beecham, Sir Thomas (1879–1961), 41
Beethoven, Ludwig van (1770–1827), 15, 95
  Fidelio, 15
  Sextet, op. 81b, 15, 89, 91
  Sonata in F for horn and piano, op. 17, 5, 12, 17, 89–93
  Sonata in C minor for piano ('Pathétique'), op. 13, 15
  Symphony no. 3 in E flat (*Eroica*), op. 55, 95, 97
  Symphony no. 9 in D minor, op. 125, 91
Belgium, 33
  see also Brussels Conservatoire
bell, 31, 35, 42, 47–8, 52–4, 55, 57–8
bell throat, 31, 41, 48, 55, 57, 69,
Bellini, Vincenzo (1801–1835)
  Norma, 38
  La Sonnambula, 95
Belloli, Luigi (1770–1817), 19
Berlin, 31, 34, 35, 39
  Berlin Philharmonic Orchestra, 72,
  Musikinstrumenten-Museum, 50

Berlioz, Louis-Hector (1803–1869), 94, 98
   Le jeune Pâtre Breton, 95
   Symphonie Fantastique, 19
Besson (horn maker), 33, 36
Blanc, J. (1829–1883), 52
Blandford, Walter Fielding Holloway
   (1864–1952), 4
Blühmel, Friedrich (*d.* before 1845), 32
body crooks, 28–9
Bohemia, 7, 10, 18, 24–5, 41
   see also Graslitz; Königgratz; Prague
Bonn, 89
bore, 27, 31, 41, 47, 48, 69, 101
   see also bell throat
Borsdorf, Friedrich Adolf (1854–1923), 21,
   22–3, 39, 44, 62, 110 n. 35, 117 n. 16
box valves *see* Stölzel valves
Brahms, Johannes (1833–1897), 21
   Academic Festival Overture, op. 80, 100
   German Requiem, op. 45, 100
   Trio in E flat, op. 40, 99–103
Brain, Aubrey Harold (1893–1955), 64
Brain, Dennis (1921–1957), 3–4, 64
brass band instruments, 22, 64, 71
breathing, 65–6
Breitkopf & Härtel, 82, 94
Brémond, François (1844–1925), 4, 20, 34,
   36, 54
Brown, Timothy (horn player), 47
Brown, William (1817–1893), 5, 49
Brüchle, Bernhard (*b.* 1942), 4
Bruckner, Anton (1824–1896), 41
Brussels Conservatoire, 21, 50
Budapest, 90
Bülow, Hans Guido von (1830–1894), 35
Burney, Charles (1726–1814), 12
Busby, Thomas Richard (1862–1933), 3, 44,
   49

Cacciamani, Raniero (1818–1885), 25
cadenzas, 72, 73–5, 76, 84, 92–3
Callcott, John James (*c.* 1800–1882), 34
Capdevielle, Jacques P. (1875–?), 72
cases, 30
Catchpole, Charles Frederick Edmund
   (1858–1886), 24
Catchpole, James (1825–1883), 49

Cavalli, Francesco (1602–1676), 7
Červený, Václav František (1819–1896), 41
chamber music, 14–16, 17
Charles, Mr (*b.* before 1710; *d.* after 1755), 14
Chaussier, Henri (1854–1914), 34
Chromatic French horn, 32
Chromatic trumpet, 32
Civil, Alan (1929–1989), 4
Clagget, Charles (1740–*c.* 1795), 32
Clinton, Charles (*fl.* late 19th century), 44
Coar, Birchard (1892–?), 4
Colin, Louis (*c.* 1785–?), 17
collections, 49–50
compensating double horn, 35
The Compleat Tutor, 51, 53, 63
Conn, G.C. (horn maker), 47
Contore delle arti e d'industria, 86, 87
Copenhagen Opera Orchestra, 69
cor alto, 11, 19, 63, 89
cor basse, 11, 12, 19, 39, 63, 64, 82, 89, 90
cor de chasse, 7, 27–8, 47, 55, 72
cor mixte, 19–20
cor solo, 29, 54, 90
corne de chasse, 9
corne par force, 9
cornetto, 9
corno, 9
corno da caccia, 9
corno da tirarsi, 9
Cornon, 41
Cöthen, 8
couplers, 30, 37
   see also master crook and coupler system
Courtois (horn maker), 48
crooks, 30–1, 34, 35, 37, 47, 54, 56, 59, 92, 94
   see also body crooks; master crook and
   coupler system; terminal crooks
Crusell, Bernhard Henrik (1775–1838), 69
cylinder valves *see* rotary valves

Daniel, William M. (*c.* 1807–?), 24
Danzi, Franz Ignaz (1763–1826), 17
   Quintets, op. 56, 17
   Sonata in E minor, op. 44, 61
Dart, Thurston (1921–1971), 69
Dauprat, Louis-François (1781–1868), 14,
   17, 18, 22, 23, 26, 90

Méthode de cor alto et cor basse, 5, 34, 45, 52, 54, 68, 70–1
  appoggiaturas, 76–7
  articulation, 77
  breathing, 65
  cadenzas, 74
  embouchure, 64
  hand stopping, 57, 58–9, 61
  lip trills, 66–7
  ornamentation, 75–6
  tone quality, 73
  tonguing, 66
  trills, 76
Delgrange, Arthur François (1858–?), 72
Deutsche Musiker Zeitung, 35
Devémy, Jean (1898–1969), 72
Dietrich, Albert Hermann (1829–1908), 101
Dolmetsch, Arnold (1858–1940), 2, 3, 69
Domnich, Friedrich (1728–1790), 13
Domnich, Heinrich (1767–1844), 10, 13, 18, 19–20
  Méthode de premier et de second cor, 52, 58, 61, 63, 66, 67, 70, 91
Donington, Robert (1907–1990), 69
Donizetti, Gaetano (1797–1848)
  L'amor funesto, 95
  Don Pasquale, 38
  Lucia di Lammermoor, 38
dotted rhythms, 77–8
  see also notes inégales
double horn, 3, 31, 34–5, 37, 41, 101
  see also compensating double horn
Dresden, 9–10, 11, 21, 25, 28, 39, 80, 81, 84, 94, 97, 117 n. 16
Duvernoy, Frédéric Nicolas (1765–1838), 18, 19, 69
  Méthode pour le cor, 19, 52, 58, 66

Eckhoff (horn player; *fl.* 1862–3), 23
Edinburgh University Collection of Historic Musical Instruments, 49
Elgar, Sir Edward (1857–1934), 1, 68, 77
embouchure, 55, 56–7, 63–5
England, 3, 11, 12–13, 16, 22–4, 28, 35, 39, 44, 48–9, 51, 71, 80
  see also London
Entraigue, Edmond (1878–1957), 54

Erzegebirge Mountains, 40
Eschenbach, Isaak (*fl.* 1755), 40
Esterházy, 13, 82, 83

F horn, 1, 3, 4, 41, 49
  see also piston horn
factitious notes, 20, 58, 90–1
Fantini, Girolamo (*c.* 1600–?), 55
Farkas, Philip (1914–1992), 67
Fentum, Jonathan (publisher), 14
Fétis, François-Joseph (1784–1871), 20
Finke, Helmut (horn maker), 48
Fitzpatrick, Horace (*b.* 1934), 4, 64, 67, 72
Förster, Christoph Heinrich (1693–1745), 9, 75
Forrest Harmony, 14
fortepiano *see* piano
France, 10, 16, 17, 29, 33, 36–7, 41, 43, 47, 48, 52, 78–9
  Garde Republicaine, 42
  National Guard, 18
  Revolution, 12, 18
  see also Paris; Versailles
Franck, César (1822–1890), 20
Franz, Carl (1738–1802), 13
Franz, Oskar (1843–1889), 62, 64
The French Horn Master, 51
Fröhlich, Franz Joseph (1780–1862), 12, 45, 52
  Vollständige Theoretisch-pracktische Musikschule, 43, 54, 58, 60, 65, 67, 73

Gallay, Jacques-François (1795–1864), 18, 19, 22, 69
  Méthode pour le cor, 52, 57–8, 66, 70
Garthwaite, F (*fl.* 1864), 49
Geminiani, Francesco Xaverio (1687–1762), 84
Germany, 4, 16, 21–2, 25, 35, 39–40, 41, 48, 49, 52, 54
  see also Berlin; Bonn; Erzegebirge Mountains; Hamburg; Karlsruhe; Klingenthal; Markneukirchen; Munich; Nuremberg; Oettingen-Wallerstein; Offenbach am Main; Oldenburg; Saxony; Weimar; Würzburg; Zittau

Glass (horn player), 100
Glinka, Mikhail Ivanovich (1804–1857), 25
Gloucester Folk Museum, 50
Göroldt, J.H. (*fl.* 1822), 52
Gounod, Charles François (1818–1893), 36,
    37, 39, 52
  Six Mélodies, 19
Grand method for the French Horn by
    Meifred, Gallay and Dauprat, 22
Graslitz, 39–40
Graun, Johann Gottlieb (1702/3–1771) *or*
    Carl Heinrich (1703/4–1759), 9
Graupner, Johann Christoph (1683–1760), 8
Gregory, Robin (*d.* 1971), 4
Griessling & Schlott, 32
Gumbert, Friedrich Adolf (1841–1906), 3,
    21, 101, 103, 107 n. 46
Gumbert-Modell, 101
Gumbert, Edmund (*fl.* 1898), 35, 101
Gumbert, Friedrich *see* Gumbert, Friedrich
Gumpert-Kruspe System, 35

Halary (horn maker), *30*, 32, 36, 48
Halévy, Jacques-François-Fromental
    (1799–1862), 20
Hallé, Sir Charles (1819–1895), 23
Hallé Orchestra, 23, 49
Halstead, Anthony (horn player), 4, 48
Haltenhof, J.G. (*b.* 1701), 29
Hamburg, 39
Hampel, Anton Joseph (*c.* 1710–1771), 9–11,
    12, 14, 28, 45, 51, 64, 81, 84
hand horn, 3, 5, 16, 18–26, *30*, 31, 34, 36,
    37–40, 48, 51–2, 57, 62, 90–2, 98–9,
    100–3
  see also cor mixte; cor solo;
    Inventionshorn
hand stopping, 9, 10–11, 12–13, 16, 29, 31,
    36, 37–8, 51–2, 54, 55, 56–62, 66–7,
    81, 84, 87–8, 92, 93–4, 101, 102–3
valve horn, 19, 21, 49, 54, 62, 94, 100
  see also cor mixte
Handel, George Frideric (1685–1759), 11, 51
  Giulio Cesare: Va tacito, 11, 79
  Water Music, 11, 14
Handley, William Huntingdon (1815–
    c. 1896), 44, 49

Harburg *see* Oettingen Wallerstein
Hardy, Henry Pope (1796–1864), 34
harmonic series (open notes), 8, 42, 54–5,
    56–7, 59–61, 81–2, 83–4, 90–1, 92
Harmonie, 15–16
harp, 17
Harper, Charles Abraham (1818–1893), 24,
    34, 44, 49
harpsichord, 75
Harvard University Library, 94
Hasse, Johann Adolf (1699–1783), 9
Haudek, Karl (1721–after 1800), 10, 12,
    84–5, 117 n. 16
Haumuller (*fl.* 1845), 52
Hawkes (horn maker), 33, 48, 49
Hawkins, Sir John (1719–1789), 13
Haydn, Joseph (1732–1809), 13, 15, 70, 97,
    100
  Cassation in D for 4 concertante horns
    and strings, 13
  Concerto in D, Hob VIId:1, 82
  Concerto in D, Hob VIId:3, 82–4
  Concerto in D, Hob VIId:4 (attrib.
    Haydn), 75, 82, 84–5
  Concerto in E flat, Hob VIId:2 for 2 horns,
    82
  Concerto in E flat for 2 horns (attrib.
    Haydn), 82
  The Creation, 15
  Divertimento à tre, Hob. IV:5, 13
  Symphonies
    No. 31 in D (Hornsignal), 13
    No. 47 in G, 78
    No. 48 in C (Maria Theresa), 13
    No. 51 in B flat, 13
    No. 72 in D, 13
Haydn, Johann Michael (1737–1806), 82
Heinichen, Johann David (1683–1729), 9
Hess, Max (1878–1975), 101
high horn *see* cor alto
Hiller, Ferdinand (1811–1885), 97
Hinchcliffe (*fl.* late 19th century), 54
Hoffmann, Ernst Theodor Amadeus
    (1776–1822), 97
Holmes, Valentine (composer), 14
Homilius, Friedrich (1813–1902), 25
Hopgood, J.F. (*c.* 1809–?), 24

horn *see* Baroque horn; cor de chasse; cor
    solo; corno da tirarsi; double horn; F
    horn; hand horn; Inventionshorn;
    omnitonic horn; piston horn;
    reproduction horns; reverse design
    horns; valve horn; Vienna horn
Horner, Anton (1877–1971), 3, 101
Hradec Králové *see* Königgratz
Hummel, Johann Nepomuk (1778–1837),
    76
Humple, Mr (composer), 14
Hungary *see* Budapest, Esterházy
hunting horn *see* cor de chasse

improvisation, 74
    see also cadenzas
India, 16
Industrial Revolution, 16
Instructions for the French Horn, 51
intonation *see* tuning
Inventionshorn, 10, 28–9
Italy, 25–6, 37–8
    see also Milan

Jacqmin, François (1793–1847), 52
Janatka, Johann Nepomuk (1800–after
    1842), 93
Janetzky, Kurt (1906–1994), 4
Jarrett, Henry (1816–1886), 23
Jullien, Louis (1812–1860), 17
Jungwirth, Andreas (horn maker), 48

Kail, Joseph (1782–1829), 14, 24
Karlsruhe, 17, 101
Kastner, Jean-Georges (1810–1867), 52
Keevil, Robert (1827–1919), 39, 49
Keiser, Reinhard (1674–1739), 8
Kenn, Jean-Joseph (*c.* 1757–after 1808),
    34
Klingenthal, 39
Klotz, Carl (1824–after 1869), 22, 67
Knechtel, Johann (*d.* after 1764), 9
Knoblauch, Johannes (*d.* 1765), 13
Knott, Handel (1888–1979), 3
Knyvett, Charles (1773–1852), 80
Königgratz, 41
Korn, F. (horn maker), *29*

Kramář, František Vincenc *see* Krommer
Kraslice, Czech Republic *see* Graslitz
Kreisler, Johannes (fictional), 97–8
Kreutzer, Conradin (1780–1849), 95
Krommer, Franz Vinzenz (1759–1831), 15
Krufft, Nikolaus von (1779–1818), 17
Kruspe, Eduard (1831–1919), 35, 101

Labbaye (horn maker), 32
    see also Raoux-Labbaye
Lachner, Franz Paul (1803–1890), 95
Lachner, Ignaz (1807–1895), 95
Lachner, Vinzenz (1811–1893), 95
Lafleur, J.R. & Sons, 39
Lagard, A. (*fl.* 1878), 45–6, 52, 65
Lambert, Emile-Florian (1863–?), 73
Lamouret, Emile (horn player), 54
Landgren, Peter (horn player), 99
Langey, Otto (1851–1922), 3, 46
Lausmann, I.A. (horn maker), 48
Lawson, Colin, 70
Leeser, R. (*fl.* 1828), 93
Leichnamschneider, Johannes (1679–after
    1725), 28
Leichnamschneider, Michael (1676–after
    1746), 28
Leidesdorf, Marcus Maximilian Josef (music
    publisher), 94
Leipzig, 8–9, 11, 21, 39–40, 81, 98–9, 101
    Musikinstrumenten-Museum der Karl-
    Marx-Universität, 50
Leutgeb, Joseph (1732–1811), 11–12, 83, 86,
    87, 88
Lewy, Eduard Constantin (1796–1846), 91,
    93, 95, 101
Lewy, Joseph-Rudolph (1804–1881), 21,
    93–4, 95, 98
    12 studies for chromatic horn and natural
    horn, 94
Lewy, Richard (1827–1883), 101
Ligner (bandsman), 42
Lindner, Adolf Julius Ferdinand
    (1808–1867), 21
Linz, 48
lip trills, 66–7
Liszt, Franz (1811–1886), 16
lituus, 9

London, 3, 11, 14, 17, 22–4, 28, 32, 34, 49, 51
  Boosey & Hawkes Museum, 49
  Covent Garden, 13, 23, 41, 49
  Crystal Palace Orchestra, 23, 44
  Guildhall School of Music, 49
  Horniman Museum and Library, 50
  Italian Opera, 24
  London Philharmonic Orchestra, 41
  London Symphony Orchestra, 1, 3
  Museum of London, 50
  Philharmonic Concerts, 24
  Philharmonic Society, 23
  Royal Academy of Music, 24
  Royal Albert Hall Orchestra, 1
  Royal College of Music Museum of
    Instruments, 50
  Royal Society of Musicians, 24
  Trinity College of Music, 49
  Victoria & Albert Museum, 50, 54
  Wallace Collection, 50
low horn see cor basse
Lund University, Sweden, 9, 10

Mahler, Gustav (1860–1911), 41
  Symphony no. 4, 1
maintenance, 45–6
Mann, Thomas Edward (1825–1897), 23, 24,
  44, 49
Markneukirchen, 33, 39–40
  Musikinstrumenten-Museum, 50
Massenet, Jules (1842–1912), 20
master crook and coupler system, 27–8
May, Johann (fl. 1765), 13
Mechetti, Pietro (1777–1850), 95
Meifred, Pierre-Joseph Emile (1791–1867),
  18–19, 22, 32, 36
  Méthode pour le cor chromatique, 5–6,
    18–19, 36, 52, 62, 63, 70, 73, 74
Meinl & Lauber (horn makers), 48
Mendelssohn-Bartholdy, Jakob Ludwig Felix
  (1809–1847), 3, 95
Mengal, Jean-Baptiste (1796–1878), 52, 63,
  67
Mengozzi, Bernardo (1758–1800), 65
Mercure de France, 12
Merewether, Richard (1925–1985), 56, 100
Meucci, Renato, 26

Meyerbeer, Giacomo (1791–1864), 20
Milan, 19, 54
Millereau see Raoux-Millereau; Schoenaers-
  Millereau
Mohr, Jean Baptiste Victor (1823–1891), 19,
  20, 34, 52
Montagu, Jeremy, 4
Morgan (fl. 1864), 49
Moritz (maker), 41
Morley-Pegge, Reginald (1890–1972), 4, 10,
  32, 44, 45
Mortellari, Michelle (c. 1750–1807), 32
mouthpiece, 27, 28, 29, 32, 41, 42–5
  see also embouchure
mouthpiece placement see embouchure
mouthpipe, 27, 28, 35, 40, 41, 47
Mozart, Leopold (1719–1787), 12, 70, 71–2,
  75, 76, 78
Mozart, Wolfgang Amadeus (1756–1791),
  15, 70, 92, 100
  Concert Rondo, K371, 87
  Concertos for horn, 12, 99
    Concerto in D, K412/514, 3, 87
    Concerto in E flat, K417, 87
    Concerto in E flat, K447, 87
    Concerto in E flat, K495, 86–9
    Fragment in E flat, K370b, 78, 87
    Fragment in E, K494a, 87
  Don Giovanni, 87
  Duets, K487, 14
  Die Entführung aus dem Serail, 15
  Marriage of Figaro, 86
  Neue Mozart Ausgabe, 86, 88
  Quintet in E flat, K407, 15
  Serenade in E flat, K375, 15
  Serenade in C minor, K388, 15
  Serenade for 13 wind instruments, K361,
    106 n. 31
Munich, 39
  Bayerisches Nationalmuseum, 50
Museums see Collections
The Musical World, 80
mutes, 10, 45, 46

Nagel, Josef (1752–1802), 13
Naldrett, William (fl. late 19th century), 44
natural horn see Baroque horn; hand horn

Nemetz, Andreas (*fl.* 1829), 33, 52
Neumann, F., 69–70
New Instructions for the French Horn, 12, 43, 51, 52, 63, 64
Nicolai, Karl Otto Ehrenfried (1810–1849), 95
Nikisch, Arthur (1855–1922), 3
nodal vents, 47, 82
notes inégales, 78–9
Nuremberg, 8, 39

obbligatos, 8–9, 11, 80–2
    see also songs with horn obbligato
Oettingen-Wallerstein, 13, 82
Offenbach am Main, 86
Oldenburg, 101
omnitonic horn, 33–4, 38
    see also Chromatic French horn; Radius French horn
open notes *see* harmonic series (open notes)
ophicleide, 2
ornamentation, 70, 75–6
    see also acciaccaturas; appoggiaturas; dotted rhythms; notes inégales; portamenti; ribatutta; trills; vibrato

Pace, Charles (*fl.* 1819–1849), 39
Pacquis, Antoine Victor (1812–after 1877), 20, 23
Paersch, Franz Friedrich (1857–1921), 23, 49
Paganini, NicolÚ (1782–1840), 17
Palsa, Johann (1752–1792), 14, 23
Paris, 7, 12, 14, 17, 20, 29, 39, 41, 52, 54, 73
    Conservatoire, 3, 5, 10, 17, 18–21, 34, 65, 72
    Museum, 50
    Paris Opéra, 54
Paxman Musical Instruments, 48, 56
Pelitti, Giuseppe (1811–1865), 38
Pénable, Jean L. (1856–?), 72
Penzel, J.C.G. (horn maker), 101
Périnet, Etienne François (*fl.* 1829–1855), 33
Périnet valves, 33, 34, 39, 49
periodicals, 5
piano, 16–17, 90
Pierpont Morgan Library, New York, 86
Pisendel, Johann Georg (1687–1755), 11

piston horn, 20–1, 21–2, 48
    see also F horn
piston valves *see* Périnet valves
Pizka, Hans (*b.* 1942), 4
Platt, Henry (1795–1871), 24
Pohle, Eduard (*fl.* 1841–1853), 98
Pokorny, Franz Xaver (1729–1794), 13
portamenti, 1, 71
Pottag, Max (1876–1970), 101
Prague, 7, 10, 14, 24, 40, 73, 86
Preatoni, C. (*fl.* late 19th century), 44
Proch, Heinrich (1809–1878), 95
Punto, Giovanni (1748–1803), 10, 11–12, 17, 19, 23, 66, 73, 90
    Concertos for horn, 5
    Quartets for horn and strings, 15
Puzzi, Giovanni (1792–1876), 19, 23, 24, 34, 54, 72, 110 n. 35

Quantz, Johann Joachim (1697–1773), 9
    On playing the flute, 65, 70, 72
    appoggiaturas, 76–7
    cadenzas, 73–4
    dotted rhythms, 77
    ornamentation, 75
    trills, 76

Radius French horn, 34
Rae, James (1792–1870), 24
Rae, John (1787–1841), 24
range *see* tessitura
Raoux (horn maker), 14, 36, 39, 90, 110 n. 35
Raoux, Joseph (*c.* 1725–before 1800), 29
Raoux, Lucien-Joseph (1753–*c.* 1821), 3, 29, 54
Raoux-Labbaye (horn maker), 4, 23, 49
Raoux-Millereau (horn maker), 48
recordings, 1, 3
Reicha, Antoine-Joseph (1770–1836)
    Quintet in E, op. 106 for horn and strings, 15
    Quintets for wind, 17
    Trios for 3 horns, op. 82, 14
Reiche, Gottfried (1667–1734), 81
Reinecke, Carl Heinrich Carsten (1824–1910), 23, 35
Reiner, Franz (*fl.* 1763), 13

Reinhardt (composer), 9, 84–5
Reinhardt, Johann Gottfried, 117 n. 16
reproduction horns, 5, 46–7, 48, 49
reverse design horns, 54
ribatutta, 76, 77
Richter, Hans (1843–1916), 41, 101
Ridgeon, John, 67
Riedl, Joseph Felix, 24, 33
Riemann, Hugo (1849–1919), 40
Ries, Ferdinand (1784–1838), 17, 89
right hand technique see hand stopping
Rimmer Collection, Wigan, 50
Röllig, Peter (c. 1650–1722), 7
Rose, Algernon Sidney (1859–1934), 22
Rosen, Charles Welles (b. 1927), 69
Rosetti, Francesco Antonio (c. 1750–1792)
    Concertos for horn, 5, 13, 34, 77, 82, 89
    Partitas for wind, 89
Rossini, Gioachino Antonio (1792–1868)
    Prélude, Thème et Variations, 19
rotary valves, 21, 25, 33, 39, 40, 49, 94, 101,
    102
Rubini, Giovanni Battista (1794–1854), 72
Rudall, Carte & Co Ltd, 48
Russia, 25

Saint-Saëns, Charles Camille (1835–1921)
    Andante for horn & organ, 19
    Morceau de Concert, op. 94, 34
    Romance in E, op. 67, 34
salaries, 23–4
Salomon, Johann Peter (1745–1815), 14
Salzburg, 12
Sanders, Neill (1923–1992), 44
Sattler, Christian Friedrich (1778–1842), 32
sauterelle, 33, 39, 49
Sax, Adolphe (1814–1894), 41, 64
Saxony, 8, 10, 11
    see also Cöthen; Dresden; Leipzig
Schantl, Josef (1841–1902), 38
Schindler, Andreas (fl. 1737), 10, 80
Schindler, Johann (fl. 1734), 9, 80
Schlesinger, Maurice (1798–1871), 17
Schlitterlau (horn player), 98
Schmidt, C.F. (horn maker), 35
Schmid, Engelbert (horn maker), 48,
Schneider, Friedrich (fl. 1817), 16

Schoen, Signor (composer), 15
Schoenaers-Millereau (horn maker), 36
Schubert, Franz Ludwig, 21, 62
Schubert, Franz Peter (1797–1828), 100
    Auf dem Strom, D943, 93–97
    Quartet in G, D887, 93
    Nachtgesang im Walde, D913, 93
    Schlachtgesang, D912, 93
Schumann, Robert Alexander (1810–1856),
    94
    Adagio & Allegro in A flat, op. 70, 97–99
    Conzertstück, op. 86, 72, 97, 98–9
    5 Hunting Songs, op. 137, 97
    Phantasiestücke, op. 73, 97, 99
Schumann, Clara Josephine (1819–1896),
    98, 101
Schuncke, Johann Christoph (1791–1856),
    69
Sedlak, Wenzel (1776–1851), 15
Segisser (horn player), 101
Selmer (horn maker), 36
Seraphinoff, Richard (horn maker), 48
Shaw, George Bernard (1856–1950), 41
Simpson, John (d. c. 1749), 51
Simrock (publisher), 102
Simrock, Nikolaus (1751–1832), 89
singing, 12, 72, 73, 74
single F horn see F-horn; piston horn
Škroup, František Jan (1801–1862), 24
slide horn see corno da tirarsi
slide trumpet see tromba da tirarsi
Smithsonian Institute, Washington, 50
songs with horn obbligato, 17, 24–5, 95
Spandau (b. c. 1750), 12–13, 51
Spitta, Julius August Philipp (1841–1894), 80
Spohr, Louis (1784–1859), 72
Sporck, Count Franz Anton (1662–1738),
    7–8, 18
Stamitz, Franz (fl. 1750–1775), 13
Standen, James William (1830–1903), 49
Steglich, Hermann (b. c. 1820), 23, 34
Stein, Johann Georg Andreas (1728–1792),
    90
Steinmüller, Thaddäus (c. 1725–1790), 13,
    83
Stennebruggen, Alphonse (1824–1895), 44
Stich, Jan Václav see Punto, Giovanni

Stiegler, Karl (1876–1932), 3
Stock, A. (d. after 1910), 49
Stölzel, Heinrich (1772–1844), 31–2
Stölzel valves, 31–2, *37*, 39
stopped notes *see* hand stopping
Stowell, Robin, 70
Strauss, Franz Joseph (1822–1905), 35, 101
Strauss, Johann Baptist, Snr (1804–1849), 38
Strauss, Richard Georg (1864–1949), 41
Süssmayr, Franz Xaver (1766–1803), 87, 90
Sweda, Wenzel (*c.* 1638–1710), 7
Sweden *see* Lund University
Switzerland *see* Zurich

Telemann, Georg Philipp (1681–1767), 11
    Concerto in D, 75
tenor cor, 42
tenor horn, 42
terminal crooks, 20, 29–30, 34–5, 36, 38, 39,
    48, 101
tessitura, 11, 55–6, 80, 81,
Thévet, Lucien (*b.* 1914), 72
Thibouville-Lamy, Jérôme (horn maker), 39
Thompson, Peter (*d. c.* 1757), 51
thumb valve, 34, 35, 37
Thurner, Friedrich Eugen (1785–1827), 17
Tietze, Ludwig (1797–1850), 93
Tippett, Sir Michael (1905–1998), 7
tonguing, 30–1, 66
Tosoroni, Antonio (1787–1855), 25
transposition, 19, 20, 34
trills, 66–7, 75, 76, 77, 81, 84
    see also lip trills, ribatutta
tromba da tirarsi, 9
trombone, 1, 24, 41
trompe de chasse *see* cor de chasse
trumpet and trumpeters, 8, 9, 24, 33, 45, 47,
    51, 55, 81, 99
    see also Chromatic trumpet; tromba da
    tirarsi
tuba, 2, 41
tubing, 56
    see also bore
Tuckwell, Barry Emmanuel (*b.* 1931), 4,
    55–6, 64
Tully, Charles (1787–1845), 6, 28, 54, 64
tuning, 28, 31, 42, 46, 48, 54–5, 81

tuning bits, 28, 47
tuning slide, 29, 42, 47
Türk, Daniel Gottlieb (1750–1813), 70, 71,
    73, 74–5, 76
Türrschmidt, Carl (1753–1797), 13, 14, 23,
    29
Türrschmidt, Johann (1725–1800), 13
tutors, 4, 5–6, 51–2, 62
    see also authors of particular tutors

Uhlmann, Leopold (horn maker), 24, 25, 32,
    35, 38
United States of America, 35, 50, 101
Urbin, Donatien (1809–1857), 52
USSR *see* Russia

valve horn, 3, 14, 16, 18–19, 20–3, 24–6, 34,
    36, 39, 48, 52, 54, 62, 91, 93, 94, 98–9,
    100, 101, 102, 103
    2-valve horn, 36, *37*, 39, 49, 52, 93
    see also double horn; F horn; piston horn;
    valves; Vienna horn
valve trumpet *see* trumpet
valves, 16, 32, 33–4, 36, 40
    see also ascending third valve; Périnet
    valves; rotary valves; sauterelle;
    Stölzel valves; thumb valve; valve
    horn; Vienna valves
Van Haute, Pierre-Eugène (*b. c.* 1834), 44
Vandenbroek, Othon (1759–1832), 51
Verdi, Giuseppe Fortunino Francesco
    (1813–1901), 26
Versailles, 7, 18
vibrato, 1, 3, 71–3
Vienna, 8, 12, 14, 15, 17, 24, 28, 35, 38, 52,
    86, 90, 93, 94, 95, 101–2
    Conservatoire, 101
    Gesellschaft der Musikfreunde, 82
    Kunsthistorisches Museum, 50
    Wiener Waldhorn Verein, 38
Vienna horn, 3, 31, 38, 102
Vienna valves, 32–3, 38, 49
violin, 16–7, 78
Vivaldi, Antonio Lucio (1678–1741), 11
Vivier, Eugène Léon (1817–1900), 19
Vuillermoz, Edouard (1869–1939), 3, 4, 72
Vuillermoz, Emile (1878–1960), 3

Wagner, Wilhelm Richard (1813–1883), 20,
     21, 23, 41, 62, 94, 99
  Der Ring des Niebelungen, 41
    Das Rheingold, 41
    Siegfried, 41; Siegfried Horn Call, 3
Wagner tuba, 41–2
Wallace, Andrew (*fl.* 1754), 14
Walsh, John (1665/6–1736), 14
Waterson (*fl.* 1864), 49
Webb, John (horn maker), 47, 48
Weber, Bedřich Diviš (1766–1842), 14
Weber, Carl Maria Friedrich Ernst von
     (1786–1826), 3
Weekes & Co, 39

Weimar, 8
Wendland, Fritz (*fl.* 1872), 23, 44
Werner, Johann (*fl.* 1750), 28
Westermann (*fl.* 1866), 101
Winch, Christopher (*fl.* 1739–1755), 51
Wirth, Adam (*fl.* 1839–1877), 21–2, 45,
     46
working conditions, 23–4
Würzburg, 21

Zelenka, Jan Dismas (1679–1745), 9, 55
Zittau, 82, 84
Zurich, 100
Zwierzina, Franz (1750–1825), 13